City of Light, City of Dark

City of Light, City of Dark

Exploring Paris Below

Valerie Broadwell

To order additional copies of this book, contact:
Xlibris Corporation
1-888-795-4274
www.Xlibris.com
Orders@Xlibris.com
38417

For me.

Contents

Acknowledgments

The willingness of Parisians to show me their underground world took me by surprise. Within an hour of showing up at the RATP (*Régie Autonome des Transports Parisiens*) headquarters unannounced, I was being whisked around Paris in an official RATP car with my very own Luke Perry-look alike press agent. David Padillay-Diaz took me to the Métro's central command center, two giant circular rooms walled in with blinking lights where engineers monitor the movement of trains racing along 131 miles of track, one arriving at every train station approximately every two minutes.

Two other RATP officials allowed me to interview them for hours at a time. I had not one scheduled appointment with RATP before arriving in France. There I was, a foreigner poking around huge systems that provide essential city services like transportation and wastewater disposal to keep residents from getting deadly epidemics. If ever there were a situation where one would expect to encounter bureaucracy, this would have been it. But to the contrary, doors were unlatched and thrown open, meetings were rescheduled to accommodate my itinerary, legends were retold. For reasons I still cannot explain, I was allowed access to places even native Frenchmen rarely get to see.

On another side of town and again without an appointment, Gilles Djéraouane of the Garnier Opera House gladly arranged a personal tour for me to see the famous basin of water underneath the theater. It is the same spooky pool that inspired Gaston Leroux to pen a story about an ugly guy who lurked below and made vexing boat getaways across a vast subterranean lake. The firemen who watch over the opera house from their onsite fire station even brought along a loaf of bread to lure the cat fish, barbel and eels who thrive in the basin so that I could see them for myself. I did and was astounded to see that indeed, three- to seven-pound fish thrive below the elegant, world-famous building.

Stéphane Mezei and the other subterranean explorers with whom I descended – all working people with nine-to-five jobs – dedicated a Monday night to take me on a tour of their deep and dark world under the City of Light. Angélique, one of relatively few women who regularly explore the underground quarries, is the last person you'd expect to see in a musty, creepy tunnel ninety feet below the surface. Tall and gorgeous with tresses of golden blond hair, her heavenly name and physical appearance posed an ironic contrast to the obvious parallel I saw between subterranean Paris and Homer's version of hell. Angélique's feminine presence helped keep my fears at bay.

That same night deep underneath Paris, "Yves," (not his real name), a very successful businessman above ground, led the way with confidence and humor. The others carried my backpack when we had to belly our way through small spaces. They made small talk with me to ward off a potential anxiety attack. When they sensed my uneasiness, they stayed close by.

Without a doubt, these urban underground explorers are a unique lot; I can't say I understand why a person would choose to spend his free time in such a dark, silent and crypt-like environment when, for Pete's sake, PARIS is just overhead! But I also found the *cataphiles* (the French word for those who prowl the underground) to be a kind, competent and humorous lot. Who would have expected to find such camaraderie in the bowels of Paris?

Indeed everywhere I went, whether the Métro headquarters, the Paris Opera House, an abandoned underground quarry or Paris' infamous sewers, people were not only willing, they sincerely wanted, to share with me the wonders of their underworld.

True, this project might have been more difficult for an unattractive male who didn't speak French and lacked tenacity. But then again, a guy probably wouldn't have had to worry about where he was going to pee ninety feet below the surface in the pitch black, nor stress relentlessly about his kids back in the U.S. I did both.

Before taking on this project I had both studied and worked in Paris at various times in my life, so fluency in French and familiarity with the city gave me an edge. On the other hand, I also had to deal with the stresses unique to being female, a mother and a foreigner researching for a project without any financial assistance. Maybe the project worked so well for me because if Paris were given a gender in a play, surely she would be female. She understood. Paris is beautiful, mysterious and unfailingly hospitable. It thus goes without saying that I could not have written this book without the help of an army of French people.

Special thanks goes to Stéphane Mezei and Paul Samat for taking me down to a quarry and for sharing their expertise; also to Stéphane for his superb photos without which nobody would have ever believed me; to Gilles Djéraouane, and the kind firemen Eric Chaput and Apban Frantz for showing me the phantom's "lake;" to all of the helpful staff at RATP's press and communications office, especially Anne Guastavino who arranged a ringside seat for me to view Métro's central command center and who shared with me her experiences as a subway conductor. Michel Dubois, David Padillay-Diaz and Guy Mizrahi each spent hours answering my every question about the Paris subway and the people who ride it. I thank the heavens for Artie Ragavan, my guardian angel who made sure that whatever went down, always came back up.

Finally, gratitude goes to two Americans, Jim Cryer and Beth Brockman, for their skillful and loyal editing. You kept the faith, even when I didn't.

VB

Come, sir, take courage and follow me! And hold your hand
at the level of your eyes! . . . But where are we?

The Persian
Phantom of the Opera

Preface

On a bright morning in May I arrived in Paris aboard Eurostar, a high-speed train that rockets to France through the only ground link between Great Britain and continental Europe since the Ice Age, the Chunnel. A thirty-year project, engineers had to burrow an average of 150 feet below the floor of the English Channel to reach a substrate stable enough to support forty trains a day. Each train carries as many as 770 passengers – the equivalent of two jumbo jets.

When the aerodynamic train approached the English coast, it plunged into the earth well before reaching the Channel, causing my ears to pop from the air compression. For the next twenty minutes, the view out the window was totally black. More ear popping from the rapid change in atmospheric pressure was the only indication that I was deep under water and ground.

Arriving at the Gare du Nord train station I rode the Métro subway, another underground passageway, to the Marais, one of the oldest and most charming districts in Paris. Just a few steps from the Saint-Paul Métro stop were my hotel and ahh – a bed. It was a fitting way to arrive in Paris – via subterranean tunnel – for it is these dark, dimly lit spaces underneath Paris that have drawn me back, time and again.

I saw Paris for the first time in the summer of 1979 and it was then that a lifelong spell was cast over me. The astounding Eiffel Tower; Luxemburg Gardens turned magical on a foggy morning; a cozy café on a cold, drizzly day; a beaded glass of cold beer at a sunny café; a stroll up the ancient *rue* (street) Mouffetard. Paris was, and is, irresistible.

But those wonders and simple pleasures were not what drew me back.

I did not know I would one day write a book, not about the delights I had enjoyed in Paris at ground level, but about my fascination with those below. Looking back now, it all makes sense. Even though most of my Paris sightseeing had been done above ground, it was the cool, dark, damp-smelling places that intrigued me. I love beautiful things and Paris is a cornucopia of beauty, but I found much more compelling the flea market of humanity riding the grimy, loud and garishly lit Métro with its pungent smell of rubber and electricity.

The summer of 1979 was also the first time I toured the Paris sewers – one of the only sanitation systems in the world that doubles as a tourist attraction. Conceived by the talented but ruthless Georges Haussmann, the same urban planner who brought Paris its wide, tree-lined boulevards under the leadership of Napoléon III, this sophisticated system was completed in 1850 and dramatically improved public health. One hundred and fifty years later, the sewers and even the flat-bottomed boats that lead engineer Eugène Belgrand designed for dredging them are still in use. Victor Hugo spent months studying the sewers for his book *Les Misérables*. In it, both scrappy street urchins and political dissidents take refuge in the sewers to escape the law and political repression.

After a disappointing fifteen-minute tour of the creepy yet poignant Paris Catacombs, I returned the next day by myself to try and absorb the enormity of so many lives lost to revolutions, massacres and plagues, and unavoidably, to contemplate the reality of my own mortality.

For centuries the Parisians mined rock and used it to build some of the world's most famous buildings: Notre Dame Cathedral, the Louvre, Versailles, the bridges over the Seine. They also discovered uses for gypsum, clay, chalk, sand, gravel and mineral water – six more exploitable resources underneath Paris. The result of all this excavation is that much of Paris sits atop more than 1,900 acres of underground caves, galleries and tunnels.

So it was that, one day in 1994, fifteen years after my first visit, my longtime Parisian friend Philippe told me the legend of beatniks stealing away with their torches to *la plage* (the beach), a sandy underground gallery deep under the Latin Quarter and it clicked. Underneath Paris there was a story waiting to be told and I would be the one to tell it. It was then that I knew I had to write this book.

Subterranean Paris tells us about the past. Indeed, it seems as though the structures below are there to ensure that one generation never forgets the struggles of its predecessors. Beginning with the Romans and lasting until the mid-nineteenth century, inhabitants used local limestone to create a magnificent city that is the number one tourist destination in the world.[1]

During World War II abandoned quarries served Parisians well. Public access points with stairs leading down to several underground galleries were built so that civilians could seek quick shelter in the event of an air raid. And while the Nazis exploited the abandoned quarries during the Occupation – maintaining a large bunker in one quarry and even a hospital in another – the Resistance had their own subterranean hideouts, too.

Underground Paris leads us to the future too, for down below ancient works crisscross with the Métro, a transportation system vital to Paris of the twenty-first century. The Métro's newest line, the completely automated Météor that opened in 1998, is the most technologically advanced system of underground transportation in the world.

Unlike any other city in the world Paris, with its abandoned rock quarries, subterranean waters, dense subway system and labyrinth of sewers, has created over the centuries a city beneath a city, each layer a chapter in the book of Paris. As the city grew and changed, these dark places were woven – and continue to be woven – into Parisian history, culture and myths.

Subterranean Paris has a history of underground mischief. Throughout the past stories have abounded about political dissidents, revolutionaries, vagrants, partying beatniks, phantoms, spelunkers and lost souls – all wandering in a subterranean city of dark under the City of Light. I climbed down to see their world and to hear their stories.

Now, so too can you. *Venez avec moi.*

Notes

[1] World Tourism Organization (www.world-tourism.org)

Chapter 1

The Cataphiles

And down I went.

"What the hell am I getting into?" I mumbled as I shakily worked my way down a manhole shaft with iron rungs set into concrete. I could not see the bottom. Descending into a pitch-black abyss with people I'd only met on the Internet was probably not the smartest thing I've ever done in my life. But it was one of coolest.

It took a lot of planning to get to this point: months of diplomacy in French to earn the trust of a secretive group of underground explorers, a bumpy flight across the Atlantic, jet lag and the expenditure of all of my annual leave at my day job. Now that I was actually about to become part of this clandestine society for a night, it came down to one single thought: I was scared.

Cataphile is the French word for someone who dwells in the underground. I would go further to say that it is an obsession for many of them. Stéphane Mezei, my contact whom I had only met in person for dinner just a few nights prior, had arranged an underground tour of the 13th *arrondissement*, or neighborhood, just for me. I met up with him and five other experienced cataphiles one Monday night on a busy boulevard near place d'Italie. They were a small representation of the roughly one thousand cataphiles who regularly go quarry diving in the Paris area every month.

By the time I had arrived at around 8:30 p.m., all six were already huddled and chatting at our designated meeting place, decked out for underground exploration. Stéphane or "Stef," had instructed me on how to dress and what to bring. I was prepared for a five-hour (Did I mention illegal?) tour of underground tunnels and galleries. I wore waterproof knee-high boots, jeans, a T-shirt and a head lamp. Cell phones are useless under solid rock, but I brought mine along anyway as a security blanket. For sustenance I packed a bottle of Evian water, bread, chocolate and a bottle of wine. I guess if you're French that's all you need to survive – explaining why nobody balked when I showed them my provisions.

After a few minutes of discussion about our route and the logistics of removing the manhole cover, it was time to make our move. While the rest of us watched from the shadows, Stef and another seasoned cataphile, Paul Samat, pried open the cover with a crowbar. Going under Paris is strictly forbidden but the police can't arrest you unless they catch you in the act, so once the cover was off we had to descend quickly. When Stef and Paul gave us the "all clear" sign, we walked smartly to the manhole and, one-by-one, all seven of us disappeared down the hatch, just like clowns in a circus act.

The author with her underground guide, Stéphane Mezei, a veteran cataphile. Photo by Paul Samat

Stef was my guide into the darkness; I had to follow him on faith. The only two things I made him promise me beforehand were that we wouldn't go through any passages so small that we had to crawl through on our bellies and that we wouldn't visit any catacombs. I had gotten my fill of skulls and bones at the official Catacombs site at Place Denfert-Rochereau. Stef broke his first promise but, thanks to *le bon Dieu*, he kept the second.

What if we get lost?

A fellow writer, Jim Cryer, had advised me before I left the States to write down the location, date and time of my descent, the names of the people with whom I would be going, and to leave it with someone above ground. I balked at his advice. After all, these guys were professionals. They maintained password-protected websites with elaborate, detailed maps of underground Paris. They posted weekly photos of their descents with the location, date and often details on the place of entry and exit. Based on my email correspondence with several cataphiles over the course of months, plus my dinner with two of them and their families a few nights prior, they seemed like a normal enough bunch, competent at underground exploration and pleasant.

But now, at the moment of descent, the common sense of Jim's recommendation came crashing down on me. I felt queasy with the knowledge that the maze of tunnels and galleries underneath Paris totals 186 miles. If we got lost, who would know we were even down here? How would search-and-rescue teams know where to start looking? Needless to say, a secret tour of underground Paris is not for the faint of heart nor the claustrophobic.

As I kept climbing down, down, down into the bowels of Paris, my imaginative writer's brain leapt forward to the scene where construction workers have discovered my shriveled up body decades later. They leaf through a tattered U.S. passport and decipher my name, "Valerie Jean Broadwell." They retrieve the tape from my portable recorder and hand it over to a museum. My story finally makes it to press in the *International Herald Tribune* and appears on the wire in newsrooms around the world. Published, finally! The only problem is that I've been dead for fifty years.

Stop thinking!

Once we had all assembled at the bottom of four sets of ladders, I pulled up so close behind Stef, my lifeline now, that I crashed into him, propelling him forward before he even got a chance to light his carbide headlamp. Though the others probably figured it out, I didn't want them to know that this plucky journalist was rather freaked out. So I focused on one image only: throwing those panicky thoughts down the sewer – quite literally in this case.

After a few minutes of tinkering and a weird burning smell, Stef, Paul and Laurent got their powerful carbide headlamps lit. The others had either battery-powered headlamps or carried flashlights. I fumbled through my backpack for my headlamp and put it on as quickly as I could. It made me feel more confident – like a real urban explorer, or maybe a miner. But I was still shaky.

"*Ça va?*" Stef asked me with a look that oozed French charm – something Frenchmen can apparently pull off even in dark and spooky places.

"*Oui, ça va,*" ("Yes, I'm okay") I managed with a feeble smile. "Being this far down underground is something I've never done before," I said, trying to sound in control. Then, under my breath in English and to no one in particular, "It's just that I'm freaked out by all this."

Indeed, it was a totally new experience for me, one I wasn't prepared for. It didn't take me long to arrive at the conclusion that underground exploration wasn't my cup of tea. Unlike a cataphile, being that far below the surface felt extremely unnatural. If there were an emergency or if I really panicked and decided that I wanted out, how in the world would I get back up? There was no quick way out.

But the memory of my crashing into Stef like a scaredy-cat Gilligan clinging to the Captain helped to brush aside that archetypal fear of being trapped and refocus on why I was there in the first place: to meet the cataphiles. Angélique, one of a small number of female cataphiles, was along just for my benefit and I was immensely grateful for her presence.

She was a striking beauty with long blond hair who, even at this depth, wore mascara, lip gloss and Chanel No. 5.

For some reason I found this wellspring of femininity in such a creepy and isolated space comforting. I stuck close to her, too.

Once assembled with head lamps on and backpacks secured, the seven of us: "Yves" (not his real name), Angélique, Alex, Laurent, Paul, Stef and I began trekking single file down a long, dark tunnel that had a perfectly arched ceiling. It was about eight feet tall but narrow enough to almost touch the wet, cold sides with both hands if I stretched out my arms. Other than the light of the headlamps, the tunnel was pitch black and completely silent. The sealed environment muffled voices and footsteps.

Angélique is one of only a few female cataphiles. Photo by Stéphane Mezei

As we started walking, curiosity about Angélique began to replace fear as I got back into my element as writer, peppering her with questions about why she is a cataphile. As we journeyed on foot through this life-sized rabbit warren, I could see zillions of dust particles floating in the column of light produced by our headlamps. I wondered whether I was breathing in some ancient microbe like the Bubonic plague or leprosy that had been sitting dormant for centuries down there, just waiting for a fresh victim to infect . . .

STOP! Don't think about it!

Without other stimuli to divert my attention from catastrophic thoughts, staying on task was a job in itself. The solution for me was to maintain a constant banter with the others so that I could focus on them, not the place.

Almost all of the people with whom I descended worked in computer technology in their above – ground lives. When I asked Yves, our hike leader, what he did for a living, he responded in English, "All of us are what you call computer geeks." Then he said no more. Obviously and for reasons yet unknown to me, Yves didn't want me asking too many questions about his and the other cataphiles' lives above ground. So I left it alone for the moment.

The one exception was Laurent, an *égoutier* (sewerman). His job was to float down wastewater canals underneath Paris in a flat-bottomed boat, clearing the canals of every kind of nasty debris imaginable. At least one book has been written about these legendary, somewhat mysterious workers who face unique dangers on the job.[1] How lucky was this? Here I was, sixty feet under Paris with six other people and one of them turns out to be one of the famed *égoutiers*! I flipped the ON button of my portable tape recorder and went to work.

Where all that rock came from: Can you dig it?

About 38 million years ago when the Paris basin was an ocean floor, marine sedimentation created layers of limestone and gypsum deposits. Geological forces and erosion separated the deposits so that limestone lies to the south of the Seine River and gypsum lies to the north of it.

Though human presence in the Paris region dates back 100,000 years to the Paleolithic Age, the Romans were the first to mine Parisian rock beginning around AD 53 after they invaded and conquered the Parisii, a Celtic tribe that were the first to settle on what is now Île-de-la-Cité. The Romans expanded the city onto the higher ground of the left bank of the Seine (when facing downstream) – an area that would come to be known as the Latin Quarter. They were skilled builders of everything: walls, baths, aqueducts, amphitheaters, roads, and found all the stone that they needed right under their Roman feet. By the eighteenth century limestone and gypsum mining was the main industrial activity in Paris. It continued until the mid-nineteenth century, providing the city with a constant source of durable building material and income.

Modern-day Paris sits at the bottom of a basin that was carved out by the prehistoric Seine. The topography of Paris climbs gently from the river in most directions, making the surrounding heights convenient natural boundaries for the fief of Paris, presently comprised of twenty arrondissements. To this day these hills, with pretty names like Montmartre, Ménilmontant, Mont Ste Geneviève, Chaillot, the Passy Heights and Buttes Chaumont are ancient topographical landmarks for residents and visitors alike. Most of the excavating that occurred over the centuries was done at the base of these three ancient hills (*monts*) of Paris: Montparnasse, Montrouge and Montsouris.

Up until the Middle Ages, the quarries were open pits. Filled in long ago however, all of those remaining in and around Paris now are subterranean – the oldest dating back to the late twelfth and early thirteenth centuries. The largest number of quarries was dug during the royal building boom under King Philippe II Auguste (1180-1223). His projects included a wall around the city, ramparts along the Seine, street paving and construction of a fortified castle just outside the city limits called the Louvre. He built Les Halles, the city's central marketplace that would function as such for about 800 years until 1979 when city leaders, in their questionable wisdom, decided to move the market out of town near Orly Airport. It was replaced with the enormous, multi-leveled Châtelet-Les Halles complex. The area has never been the same since and as of this writing, city officials have selected a design proposal to reconfigure the monster. More later on that.

Because of the abundance of limestone in the region, the majority of churches, monuments and buildings in Paris are constructed of local rather than imported limestone. Often the stone used in a structure can be traced to a specific quarry. For example, from the limestone quarry under the Hospital Cochin in the 5th arrondissement came the stone that was used to build all of the bridges over the Seine, all of the statues of Notre Dame Cathedral and a good chunk of the cathedral itself.[2,3]

All of this mining has left an impressive footprint underneath the city. Limestone was mined from quarries on the south side of the Seine: the 5th, 6th, 12th, 13th, 14th, 15th and 16th arrondissements, leaving behind underground galleries and tunnels that total over 1,900 acres. It's all there for the exploring – but only for those who are adventurous, curious or crazy enough . . . probably a little of all three.

In 1774 a catastrophic, deadly collapse of what is now boulevard St. Michel in the Latin Quarter prompted King Louis XV to order a comprehensive inventory of the quarries. Following the1776 inventory the king created the post of *Inspection des Carrières*, an office that still exists today as the *Inspection Générale des Carrières* (General Inspection of Quarries, or *IGC*). The IGC is the source of maps used by the cataphiles for their explorations.

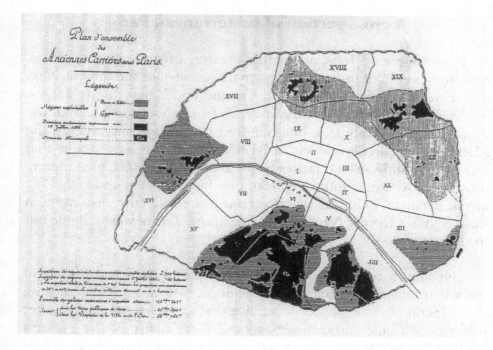

Antique map showing location of quarries under Paris. As indicated by the black shaded area, the 14th arrondissement was exploited the most heavily. Original printed source unknown.

At the same time that the IGC began mapping quarries underneath Paris, it also set about to strengthen or fill in those deemed unstable. The work continues to this day as new subway lines are added or extended, and new buildings are constructed, all which can intrude upon the underground labyrinth. In fact, the reason why Butte aux Cailles, a charming neighborhood in the 13th arrondissement still retains its village-like atmosphere is because of what's underneath it: nearly nothing. This neighborhood, perched on top of a hill with a weak and hollow substratum, simply cannot support big, heavy buildings.

A cross-section of subterranean Paris

If one were to look at a cross-section of underground Paris, beginning at about fifteen feet under the streets are the sewers. Next down are underground parking decks and under that, Métro's maze of sixteen rail lines which vary in depth from about forty feet, to the deepest station, Abbesses, one hundred feet below. Underneath the Métro tunnels are two levels of RER[4] lines – the heavier trains that serve the suburbs. The quarries begin at about sixty feet, meandering downward to a maximum depth of one hundred feet under the 14th arrondissement. Below all that is yet one more layer: the ultra-modern Éole, SNCF's (*Société Nationale des Chemins de Fer*) newest rail line out to the suburbs.

Gypsum, a type of sulfate used to make drywall and plaster of paris, was mined from quarries on the north side of the Seine. Because this mineral is a soft, chalky substance that breaks down easily under moist conditions, authorities have sealed off many of the gypsum quarries for safety reasons, thereby cutting down by more than half the exploitable areas. But when you're talking about acres and acres of pitch-black caverns and tunnels leading to who-knows-where, who's counting? Still, despite efforts to curtail exploration of gypsum quarries, the cataphiles continue to prowl those that they can get to because these cathedral-like galleries are some of the most beautiful under all of Paris and beyond.

The quarries under Paris divide into five networks, the two largest separated by the covered over Bièvre River. By far, the biggest of them is the *GRS*, short for *Grand Riseau Sud* (Large Southern Network). This huge quarry, totaling sixty-three miles, meanders under the 5th, 6th, 14th and 15th arrondissements, and connects through the southern suburbs all the way out to the suburb of Arcueil. The oldest known quarries are in the GRS under Mont Ste Geneviève and along the banks of the all-but-obliterated Bièvre River,[5] both under the 5th arrondissement.

A separate quarry under the 13th arrondissement is bordered by the Seine River on the north and east sides, and by the Bièvre River on the west. With 15 ½ miles of underground passages, this is the second largest quarry under Paris and the one that I toured with the cataphiles.

The third largest is a small network of about 4 ½ miles in length below the splendid Trocadero area in the 16th arrondissement called Chaillot. In the same area but not connected to Chaillot is another, very small quarry called Passy, named after the boulevard up above. According to Stef, although small, Passy is the most beautiful. When I asked him what was it that makes a quarry beautiful he said, "It contains the most beautiful street plaques." It figures. Parisians are always on the lookout for good art – even at these depths. Unfortunately for the cataphiles, due to security concerns expressed by banks and some wealthy residents in the area, around 2002 authorities sealed off the only access point to Passy.

Less than 400 yards in length but a bit larger than Passy is a quarry under the 12th arrondissement called Daumesnil. The area is still known among cataphiles as the "triangle of breweries" for the several underground brasseries that once thrived there.

Ranked in size then, the five separate quarry systems under Paris are the GRS, the 13th, Chaillot, Daumesnil and Passy.

Just outside of Paris, the suburbs of Montrouge, Bagneux and Arcueil – once villages distant from the city center – had huge mining operations. Unlike Paris however, since there is no law that explicitly forbids underground exploration, cataphiles take this as a "yes" and do a lot of underground trekking just outside of the city limits. The number of access points within the city varies, depending on how many manholes the IGC has sealed off and how many the cataphiles have reopened. As of this writing, there remain somewhere between five and eight manholes still open within Paris.

This constant battle over access didn't seem to concern the cataphiles. When I asked why not, Stef answered defiantly, "You can get to the GRS from Arcueil. Even if they close off all of the entry points in Paris, the cataphiles will always be able to get in from the suburbs."

We went on. After about twenty minutes of brisk walking we stopped at our first gallery. I was grateful to get to an open area where the ceiling was well over fifteen feet high. The space began as a quarry but during World War II two stairwells were installed leading down from the street so that civilians could get down quickly in the event of an air raid. Its main function now was as a party room – beer and wine bottles strewn about provided proof of that. Set up like a living room, the gallery had small tables and benches made out of smooth slabs of rock. Stef said that not long ago another group of cataphiles had staged a party here for some 200 people. It took three to four hours to get everyone down the ladders as the stairwells built during World War II had been closed off long ago. I didn't ask where 200 revelers relieve themselves but the place didn't smell like an outhouse, either. Yet another mystery to add to my growing list.

Sometimes cataphiles stage huge underground parties with over one hundred people. It can take hours to get everyone down. Photo by Stéphane Mezei

I had had some concerns about my own bodily needs before going down. What would I do if I needed to uh . . . freshen up? After all, we were scheduled to be down for about five hours. At Paul's house a few nights prior I tried to broach the question in a journalistic way. Readers will wonder, I explained. Maybe out of embarrassment neither Paul nor Stef would answer my question directly.

Still, I persisted for reasons purely motivated by self-interest. Finally, Paul's wife who has gone down a few times shrugged and said, "In a corner."

Wrong answer.

I made a mental note in my head: "Monday, no fluids after 6 p.m."

The next gallery we came to was much smaller, reminding me of a stone grotto. Like the large gallery we had just come from, it too had benches and a table. The date on the wall said 1927. The cataphiles explained that the room had been built as a break room for workers who were building a subway line above. When the Métro was constructed engineers often had to strengthen the ceilings of quarries so that they wouldn't collapse under the weight of the trains. This was one such place. In fact, much of what I saw that night had begun as an underground quarry but was later reinforced in the late nineteenth century as part of Métro construction. The tunnels connecting the galleries were much older however, as indicated in blue block letters on the wall that ranged from 1776 to 1779.

At each gallery or room that we came to the cataphiles would examine the graffiti, then usually sit down and socialize for a while. The atmosphere was congenial but nobody drank or smoked. In fact, I was the only one who uncorked a bottle of wine during our longest stop – something I felt that I needed to do in order to ante up the courage to belly my way back through a long crawlspace.

I told Stef before we went down that I wasn't crazy about enclosed spaces, particularly those that required crawling. Maybe he forgot. In any case, when I saw the others get on all fours and disappear into a hole that had the height of about a yardstick, I began to feel queasy. Amazingly, I managed to make it through the first tunnel that was about thirty feet long but I refused to go through the second, longer one that led to a gallery with a ceiling so low that an adult could not completely stand up in it. So for this second tight squeeze, the others went ahead while Stef stayed behind with me. While we were waiting in a small gallery, me sipping some wine, two other cataphiles who were not part of our expedition appeared from a dark opening that I didn't even know was there. Here we were in one of the most desolate environments I've ever been in and two guys – both whom Stef knows – come wandering by on a Monday night. The place must be swarming with cataphiles on weekends!

When the others returned from the tight gallery that I chose to skip, it was time to go back through the first crawlspace. Paul and Stef knew I was shaky so Paul carried my backpack so that I would feel less confined – yes, it was that small in some places. Stef lent me his gloves. I followed Stef, and Paul followed close behind me so that as we crawled, the two kept up a constant banter, encouraging and reassuring me that we were almost to the end. A touch of claustrophobia from first-time visitors must be something that they were used to dealing with. When I retold this part of my tour to a friend who is a therapist by day and a spelunker by night, she said that sandwiching the scared person between two experienced spelunkers while providing positive verbal cues is the protocol for getting a shaky person through a tight spot. I can't say I minded getting the undivided attention of two cute, thirty-something French guys but truthfully, that swig of red wine is what probably helped me the most.

Other than leaving themselves a few notations on the wall at places where tunnels intersected, my group was not into writing graffiti. Still, they sought out galleries known for their elaborate drawings, many of which were left by past generations. This isn't the kind of graffiti that comes from angry teenagers wielding spray cans. From what I could decipher, it was not profane nor defacing but rather portraits, collages and psychedelic reflections similar to sidewalk art. Often the graffiti contained political messages or was a reflection of the times. Some galleries had compelling human faces carved into the limestone, reminiscent of the famous Notre Dame gargoyles. I wondered how many hours . . . days . . . whoever it was that had done this, had spent underground, making their mark.

Cataphile subculture

From what I could tell there are different groups of cataphiles – each with a distinctive subculture. The "serious" cataphiles – those who descend to explore rather than to party – struck me as being more like rock climbers than beatniks. In fact, they sometimes take their camping gear down with them – everything but the tent – and spend the night. Like campers, they carried all of their trash out; a practice many other cataphiles do not adhere to as evidenced by the many wine bottles I saw strewn about. In some places there were literally mounds of trash piled in corners.

My group of cataphiles might share a bottle of wine with a snack at a resting point but their purpose for going down was to explore, not to party. They said being drunk in a quarry was too risky. They make a good point. Even with a map, moving around in an environment devoid of light and sound felt like navigation by Braille; I can't imagine trying to figure one's way out in a drunken stupor. Even if one were lucky enough to find the exit, how could a person who was even a little bit tipsy make it back up a ladder that was forty to sixty feet in length, had widely spaced rungs and in some cases, ascended on a negative incline?

The not-so-serious cataphiles only descend at entrances that are near galleries where people congregate to drink, smoke pot or take drugs. Probably the most famous subterranean party room is *la plage* (the beach) under the 14th arrondissement. Contrary to its name which means "the beach," there is no water but only a sandy floor in a large gallery with thick pillars. The walls are covered in colorful graffiti and in fact, the place was once an underground micro-brewery. In an email Stef described it to me as "a mythical place."

"The people are not dangerous there," he wrote. "The danger is only some holes and wells where you can fall if you don't see them . . . . It's really a thing to see once in a lifetime."

When I probed him further about what he meant by "mythical" he said because *la plage* gallery is not far from the entrance and so there are often groups of people congregating there. I think what Stef meant was that the gallery is more urban legend than anything else; known among partygoers because so many people have been there just to say they went underground – almost like a tourist attraction. But other than being a large underground room with graffiti-covered walls, *la plage* has no significant physical features or a history to make it unique.

Cataphiles exploring la plage *(the beach) under the 14ᵗʰ arrondissement. Once the site of an underground brewery, today it is best known as a party room.* Photo by Stéphane Mezei

A hideout through the ages

Throughout history underground Paris has served residents and invaders alike. During World War II both the Germans and the Resistance converted abandoned quarries into elaborate bunkers. A bunker built by the Germans under the 5th arrondissement called *Abri des Feuillantines*[6] (Feuillantines Shelter) had a kitchen, showers and toilets. Across town but within the same contiguous underground system the Resistance built a shelter late in the war near the Paris Catacombs that had its own power source, communication lines and enough provisions to support at least a half dozen people for days.

During the eighteenth century a number of beer makers discovered that certain quarries with a spring water source provided just the right environment for making beer. This activity was concentrated in an area called the "triangle of breweries" formed by rue Sarrette, rue Beaunier and rue de la Tombe-Issoire in the 14th arrondissement. Two of them are still accessible, *la plage*, mentioned earlier, and *le cellier* (the storeroom). The only sign left of them today are broken bottles, cement tanks and the remains of an electrical system.

"We're not lost!"

About 3 ½ hours into our trek Stef, Paul and I slowed down to take some photographs. For reasons still unclear to me, Yves and the others did not wait up. When we couldn't see their lights ahead anymore, we stopped and listened, but heard nothing. Being French, male and professional cataphiles, Stef and Paul just looked at each other and shrugged. Being American, female and a writer with the capability to imagine horrendous outcomes in mere seconds, I panicked. I began yelling "Yves!" down the long tunnel, but to no avail; sound doesn't carry underground. Stef and Paul assured me that we weren't lost but nonetheless, they did ask me if I had the map. I produced two, hands shaking, fright on my face.

They insisted that the plan was for the group to stop at a particular gallery known for its artwork. We would meet up with them there so there was no danger. As proof that we weren't lost, Stef pointed to the name of a street spray painted in light blue on the wall right next to where we stood.

When Stef, Paul and I got separated from the others, I panicked. Here Stef explains on the map where we are. Photo by Alex Roupy

"See," he said. "This is the name on the map and here it is written on the wall. I wrote this twenty years ago." Indeed, it was the same street name. I felt a little better.

After a discussion in rapid-fire French, Stef and Paul decided that Paul would walk down an intersecting tunnel to see if he could hear the others. As he turned away to start walking into the pitch black, I pleaded for him not to leave. Stef then stepped in closer, looked me straight in the eyes and said, "It's okay. WE'RE NOT LOST," rather emphatically.

While I waited anxiously for Paul to return I let out a few moans and groans, cursing the others in English for having left us behind. When Stef decided to take a few steps down the tunnel that Paul had disappeared into, I grabbed him by the shirt.

"Don't you go anywhere!" I ordered. He just smiled, probably amused at such high drama. But he did stop in his tracks and turned around.

While we were waiting for Paul to return I had recalled the story of a poor fellow named Philibert Aspairt whose body was found eleven years after he snuck down to a quarry in search of wine. The year was 1793, during the troubled times of the French Revolution. Alcohol was in short supply, which is apparently why the gatekeeper decided to go looking for an underground passageway to an abandoned monastery where monks once made a reputable wine. During those politically unstable times disappearances were common, explaining why nobody went looking for Aspairt. More than a decade later, construction workers discovered Aspairt's emaciated skeleton, eaten by rats. His remains were buried where they were discovered, under the 5th arrondissement. A gravestone marks the spot . . . but no empty wine bottles.

I imagined a marker at the intersection where I now stood; my epitaph carved into a slab of pure white limestone:

Valerie Broadwell, Writer
Lost under Paris while looking for a good story

Thankfully, Paul's return jolted me from my macabre thoughts and back to reality. He reported that the others were at the gallery where they had agreed to go to next – another indicator that these guys were pros – and were waiting for us there. So we took off down the tunnel from which Paul had just returned. Several turns in the maze and there it was, light at the end of the tunnel.

When we met up with the others I scolded Yves for having left us. "Why did you leave us?" I asked, clearly upset. "Why didn't you wait up for us?"

I don't remember Yves' response; it was only a few words, a shrug and a smile, but I knew enough not to dwell on the issue. After all, I was on their turf. So I let it go. Later that night when Stef was driving me back to my hotel he told me that Yves is a wealthy telecommunications executive, appearing on several lists as one of France's most successful businessmen. Realizing that I had scolded the French equivalent of say, Steven Jobs, I felt rather embarrassed for overreacting. But these cataphiles, including Yves, were the laid back sort; unassuming and maybe somewhat aloof. My reaction probably struck them as silly. Did the American really think that they were stupid enough to get lost?

The cataphiles insist that such exploration is safe. But having gone down, I disagree. Even during the minor episode of getting separated from the others, it took Paul and Stef, veteran cataphiles with over two decades of experience, about fifteen minutes to figure out where we were on the map and how to get to the right gallery. It is extremely easy to get lost and confused. All of the tunnels look exactly alike and there is absolutely no natural light anywhere to use as a guide. During our hike I was shown several wells that the unknowing could easily stumble into – a horrific thought. The wells are round shafts that don't seem to have anything to grab onto. I don't know how deep the water is but one would free fall at least fifteen feet before even hitting water. Worst of all, nobody would hear your cries for help.

What draws them to the dark side?

Most of the people in my group said they go down to the quarries an average of one night a week. The compelling question is, why do seemingly normal people with families and successful careers choose to spend their free time underground?

I think it is for a lot of reasons. Laurent, for example, has created an entire underground abode in a quarry near where he lives in a suburb. After a week of working in the sewers, he "escapes" to the underground for the weekend. For an introvert like him, I think the isolation is what he seeks. Others clearly go down to escape the stresses of family life or work at the surface.

When I asked Angélique why she was a cataphile she said, "I like the quiet, the calm." She added, "When I come back up I am not tired; I feel relaxed and refreshed."

Say what? She takes an underground hike in an environment devoid of light; dusty and damp, and she emerges feeling like she's been on a vacation! Without a doubt, I am not a cataphile for I crave natural light and open areas. However, in Angélique's defense, I will say that the quarries are perfectly quiet and still, a stark contrast to the roar of cars, motorcycles and sirens of the city. And once you're down there, nobody can reach you. So in that sense, subterranean Paris really is an escape.

Clearly all of the people with whom I descended enjoyed the adventure and camaraderie of underground exploration. For those cataphiles who seemed lonely or had time to burn, underground exploration offered a free and interesting diversion. Thus, depending on who you ask, the answer might be adventure, discovery, isolation, diversion, friendship or escape. But it is usually a mix. Some even descend looking for love.

As Stef had promised, our underground hike ended at one o'clock in the morning. Our way out was a shaft with one continuous ladder rather than a set of four separate ones. This required more strength and endurance than a set of ladders with landings on which to rest. And since the shaft wasn't straight, we had to sometimes climb on a negative incline, making it all the harder to hang on.

When we finally reached the top, I poked my head out of the manhole that very early Tuesday morning and took a deep breath of the cool evening air. I looked up at the stars and smiled, feeling happy to be above ground again, but also privileged to have been given this uniquely Parisian experience. Once all of us were out of the manhole, Stef and Paul secured the cover, and we began walking down the now-deserted avenue d'Italie.

We walked for about ten minutes, not saying much. There was a light breeze and I remember thinking how wonderful it felt to have my hair blown around by the wind after being in perfectly still, stagnant air for almost five hours. When we arrived at the intersection where we had to split up, I thanked my five remaining companions for coming out on a Monday night on my behalf, then bid them, "*Adieu.*" The cataphiles are an odd bunch, but that's what made them so interesting . . . and so endearing.

The street vendors don't sell postcards of subterranean Paris. Nevertheless, from that night on, the quarries and the people who dwell in them became a part of my Paris that would stay with me. Unlike the Eiffel Tower or the Louvre, I didn't have to share my memory with millions of other visitors. It was all mine.

Since then, I have noticed every manhole cover that I see in Paris and I have wondered to myself, "Is this one of the few still open in Paris?" If so, who are the cataphiles that steal away late at night to the underworld? Maybe I know them. Maybe I can steal away with them, just one more time, to the magical world beneath Paris.

Notes

1   Donald Reid, *Paris Sewers and Sewermen: Realities and Representations* (Cambridge: Harvard University Press, 1991).
2   Françoise Marie, *France: Beneath Paris* (Derry, New Hampshire: Chip Taylor Communications, 1998).
3   The majority of the stone used to build Notre Dame Cathedral was taken from quarries in Bagneux, Arcueil and Montrouge, three villages just south of Paris.
4   *Réseau Express Régional.*
5   A project is now underway to uncover several kilometers of the Bièvre River by 2007.
6   It is also called *Abri Laval* for Pierre Laval, the Prime Minister of France under the puppet Vichy government of France during the German Occupation.

Chapter 2

Le Métro

For those who go bar hopping via public transit, one o'clock in the morning is the witching hour, for that is when the last subway train of the night departs. On this particular night in Paris, my French friend Audrey and I had spent the evening downing a few beers in the lively neighborhood near the Bastille. My watch read 12:58 a.m. when we jammed our tickets into the scanner at La Bastille Métro station, then clumsily pushed our hips through the turnstiles. As soon as we were through, we took off like race horses leaving the gate, but we were laughing so hard that we only managed to limp on pathetically, nearly doubled over. We were approaching the stairs to go down to the platform when Audrey froze and listened. Yes, she had detected that familiar vacuum sucking sound followed by a rumble that gets louder and louder, signaling that a train is coming . . . the LAST train. Audrey flew down the stairs ahead of me but then, almost as an afterthought, turned back and grabbed my hand.

With a very strong French accent she yelled, "Za train eez ere!"

Unfortunately for Audrey, her accent struck me as hilarious in the way it can only to a drunk person. Now, on top of uncontrollable giggles and inebriation, whatever coordination or strength I had, left me. I was dead weight. Audrey had no choice but to drag me along like a reluctant ghost, flapping in her wake.

The train was already at the platform when we arrived. Being a native Parisian Audrey instinctively yanked down the louver of the door as soon as the train came to stop at the station. When the doors swung open we practically fell into the car, doors slamming shut right behind. Here we were, as noisy as a gaggle of girls, but nobody even looked up. At the next stop two teenaged boys stumbled onto the train in roller blades and teetered past us. I wondered how in the world they got down all those stairs on skates. When the train departed the station with a jerk both boys lunged forward as if the carpet had been pulled out from under them. They grabbed hold of the pole just in the nick of time, then they held on for dear life. On the other side of the train sat a young couple opposite one another, playing a card game on their knees. When the train doors swung open at each station a passable rendition of "When the Saints Come Marching In" wafted in from another car where a brass duo was playing for tips.

The last train of the night is always festive.

A front-row seat to Paris

The Paris Métro transports 3.5 million people a day in and around Paris and the *Réseau Express Régional* (*RER*), the rail service to the suburbs, moves another 1.5 million. Michel DuBois of the *Régie Autonome des Transports Parisiens* (*RATP*), the government entity that operates all public transit in the Paris area says, "If you want to see what Paris looks like, ride the Métro."

I already knew that, which is probably why I've always loved riding the subway. It is a front row seat to the real Paris. One of the best ways to gauge Parisian culture is to look down at shoes. You'll see clunky old lady shoes, extremely uncomfortable pointy-toed shoes with stiletto heels, strappy sandals with brightly colored toenails, stylish Italian men's loafers and a lot of fashionable pumps. The one thing you won't see is people wearing exercise shoes like Nikes or Reeboks, the ubiquitous American shoe. In France, only children wear sport shoes with street clothes. Adults do not. In France, the only time adults wear exercise shoes is when they're exercising. This great cultural shoe divide makes it ridiculously easy to spot Americans, for they are the people wearing "children's" shoes.

As a neutral observer, I find it all good fun. Parisians are not embarrassed to get on a subway train carrying a floor lamp, a bed pillow or a geriatric poodle with its midsection bandaged from front to hind legs. But exercise shoes with street clothes are a definite no-no. The one exception is young boys of African descent. In a disturbing trend, they have begun channeling black American rappers, from the perennial baseball cap and nylon jogging suit, right down to high-top basketball shoes – untied, of course – and a "I don't give a damn" slouch.

The Paris subway debuted just in time for the Universal Exposition of 1900, thirty-five years after London opened the "tube" in 1863.[1] After London's Metropolitan Railway, the Métro is Europe's fourth oldest subway system and probably the most complex.[2] Its official name was the *Métropolitain*, but residents quickly shortened it to *"Le Métro."* Line 1, as it is still called today, was constructed in less than two years. Its six-mile maiden run between Porte Maillot and Porte de Vincennes stations took place on July 19, 1900, just four months before the Exposition opened.

Today the Métro is comprised of sixteen lines totaling 131 miles served by 380 stations in Paris proper and the suburbs. One hundred Métro stations connect with either the RER or SNCF,[3] the French national railroad. The RER covers another seventy-one miles in the Paris region and has sixty-seven stations, nine of which intersect with the Métro and SNCF. Together, the two systems bring public transport to within 550 yards of every building in the city. Some of the oldest Métro stations can be spotted by their artsy entrance signs designed by architect Hector Guimard, a name synonymous with the art nouveau movement around the turn of the century.

Métro predecessors

Ever since its inception, the Métro has been hugely popular but in fact, it wasn't the first rail service in the area. During the mid-nineteenth century the Péreire brothers bought up large sections of the 16th and 17th arrondissements just after they were annexed by the city. Back then, Auteuil was an upscale village quite distant from the city. Since the Péreires owned most of the land between the village of Auteuil and St. Lazare train station, they were able to build a rail line between the two. Several more lines followed by other developers. This predecessor to the Métro came to be collectively known as the *Petite Ceinture* (Little Belt). The *Petite Ceinture* is long defunct but its creation demonstrated to the public the efficiency of intercity rail, thus paving the way for the popular support necessary for the Métro to proceed.

Even before the *Petite Ceinture* there was a train that operated between Paris and two suburbs, Le Pecq to the west of Paris and Sceaux to the south. Those commuter lines debuted in 1837 and 1845 respectively, and are considered to be the predecessors to the RER.

Remnants of the Petite Ceinture, *one of the predecessors to the Métro, can still be seen at several places in Paris. This abandoned track is at Parc Montsouris.* Photo by Valerie Broadwell

The law authorizing the French government to begin work on an intercity rail system for Paris was declared on March 30, 1898. The original plan called for six Métro lines to traverse the city, some with transfer points. Fulgence Bienvenüe, whose last name, incidentally, means "welcome" in French, was the engineer commissioned to manage the project. Before taking on the Métro he had supervised several other projects for Paris: the laying of pipes to bring drinking water into the city, construction of the Belleville funicular and carving out the whimsical Parc des Buttes-Chaumont, formerly an open-pit quarry turned garbage dump to generations of Parisians.

Rightfully, Bienvenüe has acquired legendary status among Parisians and transportation planners around the world. He led a life characteristic of the gifted: an extremely productive one punctuated by intense highs and at least one near-catastrophic low. At the age of 29 he lost his left arm in a rail yard accident. At age 46 he was commissioned to direct construction of the Métropolitain. At 57 Bienvenüe married for the first time, a widow with three children. Then in 1929, at the age of 80, he undertook the project of extending the subway to the suburbs.

One of the first challenges that Bienvenüe and his collaborators wrestled with was determining where to put the lines; the city owned only the ground beneath public roads, not that under private property. Ultimately, officials decided that it would be too onerous a task to negotiate hundreds of rights-of-way with multiple landowners. So they made the decision to build the lines under existing public streets. This decision explains, in large part, why the Métro map looks like such a mess on paper.

As one might guess, Bienvenüe's next hurdle was figuring out how to negotiate quarries, the Seine River, the Catacombs, existing regional tracks, the sewer system and other obstacles without causing anything above or below to collapse. It was obvious that the subway had to go beneath the sewers as they were right under the streets and could not be disturbed. Since the quarries were generally more than forty feet below the surface and were concentrated in roughly half of the city's twenty arrondissements, the logical place to build the subway was between the sewers and the quarries. This meant however, that in many places, particularly on the Left Bank, that the quarries needed to be reinforced so they wouldn't collapse under the weight of the trains.

Lines 1, 2 and 3 remained on the Right Bank, never crossing the Seine, but Line 4 crossed the river in two places, making a stop on Île-de-la-Cité. For both crossings Bienvenüe tunneled under the river but in other cases he went over it, especially if there was already a railroad trestle spanning the river.

Tunnels that were constructed between 1900 and 1937 were not dug as deep as those that followed in later years. During the initial phase, it was not uncommon for the subway to come in contact with the basements of private homes or businesses. Some landmarks, like the Comédie-Française theater, is well known for its "good vibrations," courtesy of the Métro below. Once while apartment hunting in Paris I went to see an elegant but relatively cheap apartment for rent on avenue Foch in the 17th arrondissement. As I walked around the apartment asking the landlady questions about the place, I could feel a definite rumbling underfoot about every two minutes. The landlady pretended not to notice. When I asked her whether the sound was a train passing beneath she responded matter-of-factly, "Yes, of course. It's the Métro!"

No . . . of course, I didn't rent the place.

Indeed, for those unfortunate enough to live right above shallow subway lines, rumbling is a fact of life, for the Métro and RER operate 365 days a year. The system operates all night long for certain events such as *Fête de la Musique* (Music Festival) every June 21, *La Nuit Blanche* (White Night) in October and on New Year's Eve. Métro trains are spaced less than two minutes apart so the wait is never a long one. The heavier, larger RER trains operate slightly less frequently.

To maintain this high level of service almost twenty hours a day the RATP employs 3,880 train conductors. Of those, 3,300 of them, or eighty-five percent, are men. That leaves over five hundred female conductors. One of them, Anne Guarardino, 37, was a Métro conductor for seven years before moving to RATP's communications office. When asked what she liked best about being a train conductor she smiled proudly and said, "The autonomy and the responsibility of getting people to their destinations."

What Guarardino liked least was working a 6 ½-hour shift with no breaks. At a line terminus conductors can take a quick bathroom break but it can't last longer than one or two minutes. However, since a 6 ½-hour workday is the maximum that conductors can work under the law, train conductors work a relatively short day for full-time pay.

Guarardino said she always felt that passengers enjoyed seeing a woman conductor, maybe because it was a novelty. I did wonder though, if this were true, why then are women so poorly represented among the ranks? There are no special requirements to being a conductor. It only takes three months of training. When queried about this, Guarardino said that a long time ago it was hard for women to get jobs as conductors, but that is no longer the case. I'm not sure I believed her answer but one theory I have is that the job of train conductor is self-selecting. Most women just don't want to work a 6 ½-hour straight shift.

When accidents happen

Most of the track repairs are done between the hours of 1:15 and 5:30 in the morning when there are no trains operating and the 750-volt current to the tracks is cut. However, some repairs just can't wait, so crews often have to work on the tracks during regular operating hours. Prior to my interviews, I had heard from several unofficial sources that the job of track repairman was especially dangerous because of the threat of electrocution or of being hit by a train. But on the contrary, all those whom I queried at RATP about this either laughed or gave me a puzzled look when I asked how often it was that a crewmember was injured or killed on the job. One RATP employee said that there may have been a death, but it must have been a long time ago, well before his tenure. These days, equipped with cell phones or walkie-talkies, repair crews are in constant contact with each other, the command center and the train conductor. There would need to be multiple communication failures for a worker to be hit by a train or electrocuted. That just doesn't happen.

What does happen with unfortunate regularity, are objects or people – either by accident or on purpose – falling from the platform and onto the tracks. When this occurs, the first thing the conductor does is shut down the train's automation and stops the train. He then notifies the central command center that a there is an obstruction on the track, and central command immediately cuts the current. Since there is no way to trip the power to a segment of track, the entire line loses power. When that happens all trains come to screeching halt, wherever they are.

The command center for the Métro, near La Bastille, is comprised of several large, curved rooms with low light. The curved walls each have several sets of lights running horizontally across them, each set being a Métro line. Facing the walls are panels with controls and no fewer than four technicians who monitor the entire network by dividing the system into four segments. The mood in the room is subdued but the technicians in their white coats chat softly and of course, smoke. James Bond or Captain Kirk would have fit right in.

What the technicians must always be attentive to are emergencies called in by the conductor or indications that a panic button has been pushed. Jean-Pierre Mary, Regulation Chief, said that the Paris subway had an average of 160 "serious accidents" each year leading to injury or death. The RATP's annual report says there were ninety-seven suicides or attempted suicides in 2003.[4] Thus, over half of the system's worst incidents are caused by suicides or suicide attempts. Contrary to what I had thought, most of them are accomplished not by impact but by electrocution. Either way, it seems that one would have to be really desperate to choose the Métro as the means to an end.

"Our role is to cut the line because the conductor has called us to say that there is a problem," said Mary, when I asked him what happens when someone deliberately throws himself onto a track. Neither he nor any of the other technicians would elaborate. But all of the veteran engineers on duty that evening nodded their heads in the affirmative when I asked whether they had experienced suicides on their watch. It seemed to me that maintaining a matter-of-fact attitude was how they coped with the knowledge that these inevitable tragedies can and will occur. Since no one can predict the when or the where, the overseers must be able to react instantly.

The power must also be cut immediately when someone jumps the tracks as a shortcut to the other side (hint: it's not worth it.), there is a fire on a train or an object has fallen onto the tracks, such as a briefcase. According to Guy Mizrahi, the public relations officer for Line 14, objects fall onto subway tracks everyday. Given that tourism is the number one industry in Paris I wondered how often it is that the suitcase of an inattentive tourist gets knocked off the platform and onto the tracks. I can only imagine the horror of watching helplessly as RATP personnel picked through one's undergarments and toiletries strewn about the track while passersby watched from the platform, furious at the anonymous tourist responsible for their delay. If it were I, would I have the courage to admit my clumsiness? *Non*.

Enter the Météor, the most technologically advanced transit system in the world. According to Mizrahi, this fully automated system that debuted in October 1998 is the world's most technologically advanced form of public transit in the world.[5] And, unlike any of the other Métro lines in Paris, neither people nor objects can fall onto the tracks because the stations have glass plates between the platform and the tracks. The doors only swing open when a train is in the station and is lined up with the doors. Other, more subtle differences between the Météor and the older lines is that the Météor stations have platforms that are better lighted, wider and have higher ceilings. Plus, there is one other big difference: all the Météor trains and stations are handicap-accessible.

Line 1, the oldest and most frequented line, is slated next for automation. Contrary to what one might think about the negative but necessary impact of automation on workers, the 800 conductors who will be displaced from their jobs will not be laid off. Rather, they will be retrained for new jobs at RATP.

"Now we have a lot of jobs in customer service that weren't there before," said Mizrahi. He admitted that moving to round-the-clock service – something RATP sees in its future – is a much less expensive proposition when there are no conductors to pay for the additional hours of service. But he qualified his statement by adding that automation requires far more specialists in communications and surveillance than a manned system. The Météor alone has seven hundred surveillance cameras. Someone needs to be watching on the other end.

The present Météor has eight super-modern stations strung along its five miles of track. In 2005 work began to extend the line under rue Tolbiac and place d'Italie in the 13th arrondissement and out to Villejuif, a suburb to the south of Paris. When Mizrahi informed me of RATP's plans I wondered at the time whether the quarry in which I had just gone exploring with the cataphiles two days earlier would be obliterated in a year. As it turns out, it was not disturbed because the quarry under the 13th arrondissement is well beneath the Météor. In fact, the cataphiles were able to sneak up to the construction site from the quarry beneath.

So for the time being, at least one quarry has been left undisturbed, while others will inevitably be lost to development. I try to remind myself that this is the reality of growth – sustainable growth, in fact. Because Paris is one of the most densely populated cities in the world, there is nowhere else to go but up or down in the urban core. Maybe one day the RATP will have to build an above-ground monorail to supplement the subway. But for now, and with a history of digging, French engineers and planners are going to continue to burrow underground. As the public transportation system expands to accommodate an ever-growing population, I imagine a future in which the cataphiles' fascinating subterranean world exists only in memory as new infrastructure reclaims these ancient spaces.

Indeed, all signs indicate that expansion is warranted.

"The trains coming into Gare Lyon and Châtelet are all saturated. The Météor was built to relieve this pressure. But we have to find ways to accommodate the growth," said Michel DuBois of RATP's press office. Another unexpected development is that for the last three years there has been the same number of passengers riding the Métro on Saturdays and Sundays as during the week. Shaking his head and sucking in air through his mouth DuBois added, "From January 2004 through August 2004 Métro ridership went up three percent and RER ridership increased ten percent."[6]

Those statistics are borne out when you look at station usage. Serving 27 ½ million passengers a year, the St. Lazare Métro station is the busiest subway station in Paris. Montparnasse-Bienvenüe is the second and Gare du Nord is the third most frequented. Châtelet Les Halles, the system hub underneath the heart of Paris, is the O'Hare Airport of public transit. A half million passengers a day bustle through this gargantuan people mover, making it the new crossroads of Europe where five Métro and three RER lines converge. The underground complex – a small city in itself – extends a half mile from the Right Bank of the Seine River opposite Île-de-la-Cité, all the way to rue Étienne Marcel.

A target for terrorists

Intersecting at Châtelet-Les Halles, Line B provides transit from Charles de Gaulle airport to the center of Paris and is the busiest of all the RER lines. In July 1995 it was the target of one of the deadliest terrorist attacks in Paris history. Seven people were killed and eighty were injured when a bomb planted under a seat detonated during evening rush hour as the train was stopped at the St. Michel Notre-Dame RER station. According to news reports, it was a grisly scene. A nearby café was transformed into a makeshift field hospital as paramedics performed emergency amputations on several of the victims. The plaza in front of Notre Dame cathedral became a landing pad for med-evac helicopters.

That year there were a series of attacks in or near subway stations, but none of the others were deadly. Then, in December 1996 there was another deadly attack at the Port-Royale Métro station, just two stops down from St. Michel Notre-Dame, in which two people were killed and more than eighty injured. All of the bombings were the work of *Groupe Islamique Armé* (Islamic Army Group or *GIA*), the radical Algerian Islamist group that wants Algeria to become an Islamic state. The *GIA* is opposed to France's support of the secular de facto dictatorship put in place after the 1992 Algerian elections.

No doubt, the large number of people concentrated in known places at predictable times is why public transit has always been targeted by terrorists, and not only in France. There haven't been any major subway attacks since 1996, but France's intelligence community eventually tracked down Khaled Khelkhal, chief of the Algerian terrorist cell operating in France, and killed him in a shootout. But even well before the 1995 and 1996 subway bombings, France had initiated an anti-terrorist program called *Vigipirate*, a program somewhat analogous to the color code system used in the United States to indicate the level of risk for a terrorist attack. In France, each level triggers additional measures such as removal of trash receptacles from streets, greater patrolling of airports, railway stations and public monuments, more random identity checks in the street, parking restrictions and the closure of some entrances/exits to public spaces.

Michel DuBois admits that the Métro and RER are so large and dense that regular inspection of all 380 stations just isn't possible. Instead, the RATP takes what he described as a "broad approach" of limiting entries and exits, and encouraging passengers to be observant. The RATP has installed metal cages underneath all of the RER train seats to prevent would-be terrorists from planting bombs there.

Because several of the GIA bombs were hidden in trash receptacles, the containers have been either removed from subway stations altogether or redesigned such that a bomb large enough to inflict major damage cannot fit through the opening. In October 1995 a bomb that had been planted in a trash can just outside the Maison Blanche Métro station didn't do nearly as much harm as intended, thanks to an alert passerby who saw something suspicious in the trash can and reported it to the police. Although police immediately cordoned off the area, the bomb detonated before experts could defuse it, and the blast injured several policemen. But the scene could have been much worse.

Yet, even with these precautions in place, authorities remain vigilant. One Parisian told me, "Not a week goes by when trains aren't stopped because of a suspect package."

About fifteen hundred public safety officers patrol the Métro, RER and buses, but passengers won't necessarily notice them as many are in plainclothes. The RATP force and municipal emergency response teams periodically stage mock catastrophes, simulating anticipated injuries and rescue scenarios. DuBois said that it takes security personnel about ten minutes to arrive after an emergency has been reported. Typical emergencies include heart attacks, fights, an unconscious drunk or a lost child. When I asked DuBois how often a child gets lost in a station or left on a train he said, "Rarely . . . . Once every five or ten years."

As for those pesky pickpockets, despite what every Paris guidebook will tell you, RAPT officials insist that they are not a big problem. The pickpockets on the trains tend to be kids who work as a group – one or more creating a distraction while the other goes for the wallet. David Padilla-Diaz of RATP's communications office tried to put it in perspective: "Yes, pickpockets are a problem wherever you have a lot of people. But the problem is not any worse on the Métro."

Once, while climbing the long spiral staircase of Les Abbesses Métro station I heard a woman's voice echo from above me, "*Au voleur! Au Voleur!*" ("Stop the thief!"). By the time I reached the top of the stairs – less than five minutes after I had heard the woman's call – four policemen were already on the scene and had cornered the offender: a boy of about ten years old. Standing beside him was his accomplis, a rough-looking woman in her twenties. Neither took the capture seriously, especially the woman, who responded to all the attention with a smirk. The French say that the pickpockets and purse snatchers are Romany gypsies. I have often wondered where the gypsies live or whether the children even go to school. One thing is certain though: their trademark is to send children to do the pickpocketing since under French law, those under ten years of age cannot be arrested nor charged with an offense.

I have lived in Paris at several different times in my life and never owned a car there. Rather, I took the Métro everywhere, everyday. On a recent visit I was pickpocketed while in a Métro car at Gare du Nord, the most notorious station for pickpockets. Gare du Nord is a rough part of town but I had good luck with me: two undercover policemen were positioned on either side of me and caught the thief, red-handed. Two hours and one official complaint later (so that the police could prosecute), I was back on my way again, no poorer for having been pickpocketed. But I was lucky, no doubt. The police told me Japanese tourists are the most frequent victims of pickpockets because they come to Paris naïve about street crime and carrying wads of cash.

There have also been a few times when I noted a group of scruffy, pre-teens moving in on me while standing on a crowded train. When I became aware of their presence I took a combative body position – elbow at the ready to inflict serious pain – and clutched my handbag close to my body. After they could see that I knew of their intentions, the group moved off. Surprise is a pickpockets' secret weapon so passengers who remain aware of who is around them, especially on a crowded train, have essentially disarmed potential thieves without saying a word nor brandishing a weapon. Sometimes, just giving them the evil eye is enough.

The homeless are another group often seen in the Paris subway. Although they might smell unpleasant, they are generally harmless.

The RATP's official position is that the itinerant are prohibited from living or congregating in the subway. Nevertheless, it is not uncommon to see them begging for money or sleeping on benches or on the floor of subway stations. Like most big city dwellers, Parisians accept the homeless as a fact of urban life. There is a benevolent association for the homeless called *L'Espace Solidarité Insertion* (*ESI*) that every night sends a bus around to the subway stations most frequented by the homeless like Gare du Nord, Nation, République and St. Lazare, and offers them a free ride to a shelter. A Parisian friend once mistakenly got onto one of the *ESI* buses, thinking it was the Number 91 from Bastille to the Marais district. It didn't take long for those more shabbily dressed to size her up and determine she was not one of them but rather, a commuter who had made a tactical error. The busload of vagrants smiled politely then shook their heads "No," signaling her to get off. Not long after she had taken her seat, a RATP official came running over to wave her off the bus.

Station themes, French flair

Indeed, some subway stations are so attractively designed that you might want to linger even if you have a fixed address. Perhaps the most scenic of them is Bastille, part of which straddles the Bassin Arsenal, allowing passengers a postcard-perfect view of this shimmering canal with quaint houseboats moored along its banks. Bastille is also one of the most interesting stations for French history buffs. While constructing the station early in the twentieth century workers uncovered the foundation of Liberty Tower, one of eight towers of the Bastille prison, built originally as a fortress to protect the city. Long a symbol of the king's absolute power over his subjects, the prison was the target for revolutionaries on July 14, 1789, marking the start of the French Revolution, a national holiday now known as Bastille Day.

Archeologists moved the tower foundation and rebuilt it in a square across from Pont Henry IV, while architects had the genius to mark the outline of the tower within the station itself so that it would never be forgotten.

"It's not a big thing to look at. It's just a yellow line on the floor," said the RATP employee at the Bastille ticket window when I asked him where it was. He was correct from a visual point of view. If you don't look for the line you'll miss it. But the fact that the French went out of their way to preserve the mere outline of the Bastille is a powerful statement about how strongly they revere their independence from monarchical rule. In addition to preserving the tower outline,[7] the Bastille Métro station has five colorful frescos painted on the station walls that tell the story of the French Revolution.

A yellow line on the floor of the Bastille Métro station marks the original foundation of the Bastille fortress where the French Revolution began. The cocquille *(shell) chair was designed to discourage sleeping in subway stations.* Photo by Valerie Broadwell

Station names run the gamut – from famous people like writers, scientists, diplomats and saints; to monuments; to places like ancient villages or battlegrounds. Some, such as Marcadet Poissoniers, Barbès-Rochechouart, Trinité d'Estienne d'Orves, Réaumur Sébastopol and Villejuif Paul Vaillant-Couturier, are a pronunciation nightmare for non-French speakers. Better to buy a map and just point.

Michel DuBois explained that the idea to give Métro stations cultural or artistic themes originated with French writer André Malraux. In1967 he made a successful case to RAPT that the Métro stations should reflect French culture and history. But even before Malraux's pitch, some stations already had unique themes, such as the classy Franklin D. Roosevelt station. Renovated in 1952 with private funds, it has a sleek and modern Art Deco look, reminiscent of a 1950s American diner.

Nevertheless, don't expect to experience French flare in all of the stations, nor even in the majority of them. In fact, the decor, or absence of, can be a telltale sign of when a station was built. The stark Sentier Métro station, for example, was built during the Great Depression when there was only enough money to build a no-frills stop. Sometimes a private donor will fund the design or the revamping of a station. Other times the government covers the cost or it could be a public-private partnership, depending on what landmarks are in the neighborhood that feeds into a station.

Music is part of the RATP's grand scheme, too. Each year about one thousand performers audition for the 350 licenses issued to buskers, or subway performers. Although buskers earn little – forty to seventy Euros a day – they know that music executives ride the Métro. In June 2003, an RATP association released the first-ever busker album entitled *Correspondances* (Connections). Two of the fourteen musicians on the album subsequently signed recording deals. They weren't the first to get their big break playing in the Métro. Musicians Khezia Jones, Alain Souchon, Shola Hama and Ben Harper were all discovered while playing underground.

From my own unofficial survey of RATP employees in which I asked them which are the most famous Métro stations, Concorde, Franklin D. Roosevelt, Bastille, Assemblée Nationale, Louvre-Rivoli, Luxembourg (RER station) and Arts et Métiers were most often cited. Les Abbesses station near

Montmartre is frequently deemed the most beautiful for its colorful murals that line a dizzying spiral staircase. One hundred feet below the surface, Les Abbesses is the deepest Métro station, so be prepared to climb; the staircase has 104 steps. If you don't want to climb there is an elevator the size of a small bedroom, but if you take the elevator you'll miss the murals.

Serving the U.S. Embassy, Concorde has ceiling and wall tiles that spell out France's *Déclaration Universelle des Droits de l'Homme et du Citoyen* (Declaration of the Rights of Man and of the Citizen) in giant letters. So those who get bored while waiting for a train at the Concorde stop can try piecing it together.

Paintings along the spiral staircase leading up from Les Abbesses Metro station. Photo by Valerie Broadwell

Waiting passengers can try to interpret the meaning of the words cast upon the walls at the Saint-Germain-des-Pres station. Called the "literary station," its whitewashed walls are made to resemble blank pages in a book. Spotlights cast single words here and there onto the walls as typeset. Another station in the Latin Quarter, Cluny-La Sorbonne, has giant signatures of famous writers scrolled onto the ceiling.

With its snappy red, white and blue theme, a lot of American tourists probably think that the Cadet Métro station is a dedication to the United States. Alas, it is not. Situated above rue Lafayette, Cadet recalls the story of the Marquis de Lafayette who fought alongside the American revolutionaries in their battle for independence. The Assemblée Nationale station serves France's House of Parliament.[8] The station walls are decorated with giant silhouettes of the human face in primary colors, presumably to represent France's diversity of people and culture.

Riders who get bored waiting for a train at the Concorde Metro station can read the ceiling. Photo by Valerie Broadwell

Several stations, like Tuilleries, Hotel de Ville (Paris station) and the Luxembourg RER station, have huge panels that explore a particular topic, often related to whatever is above at street level. Tuilleries depicts historical events of the twentieth century; Hotel de Ville tells the history of the Métro. The Luxembourg RER station has an ecology theme depicted on huge, colorful panels.

Redesigned in 1994, one of the most distinct stations is Arts et Métiers on Line 3. With walls of shiny, riveted copper and even portholes, the concept clearly came from a Jules Verne novel. The metal-toothed ceiling juts downward, like a giant beast biting down on the station and its inhabitants. Guy Mizrahi, public relations officer for the Météor, called the design "a modern response."

The elegant Louvre-Rivoli Métro station has classical art displays, perhaps so that tourists heading for the world-famous museum will know they're at the right stop. I had always thought that the statues, paintings and ceramics were authentic. When I asked Michel DuBois to confirm my assumptions he informed me – clearly struggling to contain laughter – that the art pieces in the station were replicas.

Okay, so they're not real. But the mini-museum nevertheless provides commuters with quality food for thought while they wait for a train or tourists a tantalizing taste of what it's in store just above.

Ironically, one of the most interesting Métro stations is one that has been closed for over sixty years. The St. Martin subway station was sealed off in 1939 but that doesn't stop the cataphiles and other urban explorers from entering. Just a few hundred yards from the République Métro stop, this abandoned station remains in a World War II-era time warp. In fact, it is so well preserved that it has been used as a movie set. About seven years ago during a cold snap when the temperature hovered around 20°F for two weeks, the RATP was pressured to open it up for the homeless. The request sparked a debate about the lack of proper housing for those who have none. Eventually, when better accommodations were found the station was closed once again but as a result, it shows signs of habitation.

Dated advertisement at the closed St. Martin Metro station. Photo by Stéphane Mezei

Those brave or crazy enough to run down live tracks carrying 750 volts sneak into St. Martin via the République Métro station. As soon as a train passes the platform they jump onto the tracks and run in the direction of the next oncoming train – which will arrive in under two minutes. Hopefully, they make it to the intersecting tunnel that leads to St. Martin and dive in before a train comes barreling down the track. I didn't ask what happens if they don't make it or if one trips and falls onto the track. A game of subway "chicken."

Stef Mezei, one of the cataphiles who usually sticks to quarry diving, explained first-hand how it is done, "We had to jump to avoid the electric rails . . . It's very, very dangerous."

"No kidding." I wrote back to him in my typical sarcastic humor. "One trip up and you're fried to a crisp."

In a response he quipped, "But nobody became black and full of smoke." Then he added, "Do you want to try to do the same?"

I politely declined, concluding that much of American sarcasm is lost in translation.

In the spotlight

I did however, politely respond to questions posed to me by many RATP staff about American politics. Coming from the U.S. where the 2004 presidential election had polarized the country as none before, I was taken aback and refreshed by such directness. The cataphiles avoided the subject altogether. But during sit-down interviews those in official positions had no qualms about putting me on the spot once we got past the formalities.

For example, Jean François Mahe, Regulation Chief for the RER Line B, answered all of my technical questions and then politely posed for photos. My camera was still warm from the flash when he turned to me and asked, "What about American politics? Do you think Bush will win?"

When the other eight or so technicians who were mingling around the control room overheard Mahe's question they smiled uncomfortably, squirmed a bit, then moved in closer to hear my answer. When I responded to Mahe that I hoped Bush would not win again my audience smiled broadly and let out an audible sigh of relief.

Luke Perry-lookalike David Padilly-Diaz was the press officer assigned to take me to see the Métro central command center near Bastille, as well as the RER's headquarters at Denfert-Rochereau. He, too, wanted to talk politics. As he wove our RATP minivan in and out of Paris rush hour traffic like a Monaco Grand Prix driver, he lectured me on U.S. foreign policy. His grandfather is Cuban and he remains in contact with relatives both in Cuba and in Florida.

"What do you think about Bush?" he asked in the middle of a dicey lane change. Before I could answer he continued, "Bill Clinton was the best president because he maintained a dialogue with Cuba. Now there is nothing."

I agreed wholeheartedly with his assessment, but at that moment I would have said anything to appease Diaz as long as he kept his eyes on the road. I recalled that all 42,000 RATP employees ride the Métro and RER free. Immediate family members ride for half-price.

"Good thing," I thought to myself. "One less crazy driver on the road."

Most French people commuting into Paris are wise enough not to drive into the city. Traffic generally flows, but it does so in fits of aggression, like a shark feeding frenzy. The scene is so chaotic and parking so scarce, that it is hard to imagine why anyone would ever want to drive into the city. For this reason, I found it surprising when Michel DuBois told me that, despite saturation of several subway lines – indicating off-the-charts ridership – RATP's main competitor is single occupancy vehicles or "SOV" for short. The reason for this is that as Paris sprawls, albeit at a much slower pace than an American city, those living in the most distance suburbs prefer to commute via the comfort and convenience of their own cars, but only if they have a place to park at their destination, that is.

While we were stopped at a red light, Diaz revving the engine, he explained that RATP's top three goals were: to offer affordable public transportation, to provide a safe environment and to create a pleasant atmosphere or, as Diaz put it, "an ambience that passengers like." (I guess he wasn't thinking about his passenger at the moment). He said since those who commute by SOV do so for comfort and convenience, RATP's best strategy was to offer the same level of comfort and convenience.

Well, almost.

It is true that Paris subway stations are loaded with character, especially when compared to their drab, utilitarian American counterparts. But still, the system sorely lacks basic amenities such as public restrooms and drinking fountains – to the distress and discomfort of many a tourist. Furthermore, if more Métro stations had elevators probably a lot more tourists would be able to take the subway from the airport to the city, thus alleviating some of the airport traffic. As it is, the stairs remain a formidable obstacle to travelers with luggage.

France's *Doctrine Impassable* of 1975, analogous to the Americans with Disabilities Act, requires that new facilities be handicapped accessible and that businesses provide reasonable accommodation when possible. But because the Métro predates these laws by more than a century, and the infrastructure in many cases cannot structurally support retrofits, the number of Métro stations with elevators is dismal. Out of 380 stations only nineteen of them have elevators. The RER does much better on that score: forty-nine out of sixty-seven stations are equipped.

Heat, too, is a problem in the summer, although Michel DuBois said that the number of hot days in Paris doesn't justify the expense of air conditioning. Those who survived the summer of 2003 would probably disagree. In August of that year a prolonged heat wave killed over one hundred people in the Paris region alone. When it is pleasant or even cool outside, subway stations are almost always warm and stuffy inside. If the mercury rises to above 80°F the stations can be miserable and the trains torturous. Nevertheless, for economic reasons, the RATP's only plans are to install fans so that eventually the entire system will have circulating air. That is the best it's going to get.

Most stations have some seating, but rarely enough. The prototypical seat is a molded plastic model called *la cocquille* (the shell). They're not exactly an ergonomic design, but these hard, rounded seats do accomplish their mission, which is to discourage people from sleeping in them. Then there are those platforms that don't have any seating at all. I've often wondered what the disabled, aged, pregnant, suddenly sick or otherwise infirm do under these circumstances. It seems to me that if RATP wanted to compete with cars, the first place to start would be seating.

For tourists, however, the biggest problem is not seating, but the lack of public restrooms at Métro stations. When queried about the dearth of facilities, David Padilly-Diaz said that all of Métro's public restrooms were closed for security reasons and for sanitation. He cited, *le trafic,* the French word for contraband dealing. The only stations that have full-service albeit "pay-as-you go" public restrooms are the six that are mainline SNCF stations: Gare Saint-Lazare, Gare Montparnasse, Gare du Nord, Gare de l'Est, Gare du Austerlitz and Gare du Lyon.

Some of the busier subway stations like Bastille and Étoile have port-a-johns at street level called *sanisettes*. They are those metal, space age-looking capsules on street corners. After each use they are automatically sanitized with a disinfectant, sprayed practically from ceiling to floor. Passengers who are disabled or have strollers may not even be able or want to maneuver up the stairs to get to these. In addition to being a poor substitute for a real restroom, the sanisettes can actually be downright dangerous for someone under one hundred pounds. Before the manufacturer got the wrinkles ironed out, a small child was badly burned from disinfectant when the weight scale built into the floor didn't detect him. After the toilet was flushed the urban outhouse was automatically sprayed down, kid included, from head to toe. The problem has since been fixed.

There are plans for both Métro and RER to continue expanding: Métro with extension of the Météor line and eventual automatization of all the lines; the RER will be expanded ever further out. But despite ridership levels that are the envy of many transportation planners in other places, the city is still extremely congested. One can only imagine a Paris completely choked by fumes and traffic if it weren't for the city's savior: Le Métro.

"There is no public transportation system in the world that makes money. It's impossible. Everywhere you have public transportation you need to have public funds," explained Michel DuBois when I asked him whether the system made money. Then he added, "But of course the Météor operates more efficiently so the cost is lower to the community than the other lines."

With some experience in transportation planning I try to draw from this and apply it to my own country. In most American cities, getting public support for transit is an uphill battle. I remembered what DuBois had said earlier, that the passengers riding public transportation in Paris are a faithful cross-section of the entire region of Île-de-France.[9] This probably explains why the French don't object to their tax Euros going toward transit. Everybody uses it.

By the time I got to the Métro command center, my last stop, it was 7:00 p.m. It had been a long, exhausting, but fascinating day. From morning 'til night, RATP officials granted me unlimited time to interview them. They whisked me around the city so that I could see the brains behind the trains. RATP representatives gave me their business cards and scrolled their personal cell phone numbers on them for me to call in case I had additional questions. Michel DuBois issued me a three-day pass, allowing me free reign to photograph in stations and trains. I was enormously grateful and still am amazed at how such a large agency manages to remain so accessible, even to a lone American writer.

After our interview, my last of the day, David Padilly-Diaz and I decided that it would be faster for both of us if he dropped me off at the nearest Métro station rather than him drive me across town to my hotel through the remnants of rush hour traffic. Métro would get me to my destination faster . . . and more likely in one piece. When we arrived at the Bastille Métro station we shook hands and bid each other farewell. It was a chilly September evening so as soon as I shut the door to the minivan, I bounded to the stairs and quickly skipped down to the station, where I knew it would be warm.

Déja vu

As I passed through the turnstile and entered the station, my attention was drawn to two teenage girls not far ahead of me, clinging to one another in a fit of laughter. Caught in the wind tunnel effect of the subway corridor, they were but a silhouette of blue jeans and wildly blowing hair. The scene reminded me of Audrey and I, running for the last train late one summer night through this same station. Far off, from a place unknown, I heard the nostalgic tune of an accordion echoing from a corridor. For a moment a wave of déja vu washed over me, transforming me to another century. Surely I lived here then, and I rode the Métro alongside Ernest Hemingway, James Joyce, Gertrude Stein, Ezra Pound and the others from the Lost Generation. I remember it.

The click-clack of high heels against the shiny black concrete floor jolted me back to the present. A plethora of fashionable footwear also reminded me that my own shoes gave away my nationality. Still, nobody took notice. When I arrived at the platform the warm, pungent smell of rubber and electricity hit me like a freight train, signaling to my senses that finally, I was going home. I wanted to celebrate.

Surely any train – not just the last one – can be festive. You just have to look for the party.

Notes

1. New York City's subway debuted four years after Paris on October 1904.
2. The Glasgow and Budapest subways both debuted in 1896.
3. *Société Nationale des Chemins de*
4. *Fer "Les Statistiques Annuelles"* 2003, RATP.
5. Barcelona and Copenhagen have fully automated systems as well.
6. For comparison, New York City's subway ridership has been growing at about the same rate of three percent per year. Source: Larry Hirsch, MTA New York City Transit.
7. Located on the platform of Line 5, direction Bobigny.
8. The Assemblée Nationale is the lower, directly-elected House of Parliament. Members are elected to five-year terms in constituencies determined by population. The system corresponds most directly to the British House of Commons
9. The one exception are buses which tend to have a higher percentage of women and seniors.

Chapter 3

Making Waves
The Phantom's Lake and Other Subterranean Waters

Paris sits in a giant bowl of clay and limestone that was carved out by the Seine River millions of years ago. The relatively impervious clay floor traps spring water and rain in a giant aquifer called *le nappe phréatique* in French. This layer of water under most of the region explains why, just about anywhere in Paris, if you start digging you'll eventually hit water.

Water, water everywhere. With many natural springs in and around the city plus two major rivers, Paris is rich in this natural resource. Parc Montsouris is the site of one of the largest underground water reservoirs in Paris. Photo by Valerie Broadwell

Paris has two major rivers, the Seine and the lesser-known Marne. In addition, the region is blessed with dozens of springs and artesian wells.[1,2] Nevertheless, for centuries water-borne diseases killed millions of Parisians for although plentiful, the water hasn't always been safe for drinking. In 1854 Paris chief of reconstruction, Georges Haussmann, charged Inspector General of Water and Forests, Eugène Belgrand, with the task of solving the city's water quality and distribution problems. Still in place today, Belgrand designed a plan to bring in water from pristine sources located safely upstream of the city via covered aqueducts.

Once it reaches Paris, the water is stored in five separate reservoirs in the neighborhoods of Saint Cloud, Les Lilas, Ménilmontant, Montsouris and L'Hay-les-Roses. Six other reservoirs were built to hold non-potable water used to hose down the sidewalks and to water the city's many public gardens. Some of the reservoirs are completely below street level, while others are buried but elevated. Only the trained eye can spot them as a grassy knoll, usually in a city park. At least one of them, the colossal Montsouris reservoir under Parc Montsouris, has been designed a historic landmark.

Beginning with the Romans who built the Arcueil aqueduct to bring in fresh water from the Rungis Plain (where Orly Airport is now), to the reservoirs and canals[3] constructed under Napoleon III, Paris has seen its share of water management projects – many of them landmarks in their own right. Nevertheless, arguably the most famous body of water in Paris exists only in the imagination of millions as a foggy lake underneath the Paris opera house. This lavish complex, better known as the Palais Garnier (Garnier Palace) after its young architect Charles Garnier, is located just across from the Bastille memorial and is the setting for Gaston Leroux's play, *The Phantom of the Opera*. Leroux's romantic thriller and subsequent blockbuster musical is the story of a disfigured man living in the bowels of the opera house who falls in love with the theater's main attraction, Christine.

The phantom's dreamy hideaway is on the edge of a spooky, cavernous lake underneath the opera house. Ever since the play, the lake of the opera has remained the subject of much discourse as to whether it exists or not. Here the Persian, a theater hand, describes hearing the phantom's voice for the first time over the lake:

I had no sooner put off from the bank than the silence amid which I floated on the water was disturbed by a sort of whispered singing that hovered all around me. It was half breath, half music; it rose softly from the waters of the lake; and I was surrounded by it through I knew not what artifice. It followed me, moved with me and was soft that it did not alarm me. On the contrary, in my longing to approach the source of that sweet and enticing harmony, I leaned out of my little boat over the water, for there was no doubt in my mind that the singing came from the water itself. By this time, I was alone in the boat in the middle of the lake; the voice – for it was now distinctly a voice – was beside me, on the water . . . . I shook my ears to get rid of a possible humming; but I soon had to accept the fact that there was no humming in the ears so harmonious as the singing whisper that followed and now attracted me.[4]

Is there really a lake under the opera house? Yes and no. There is indeed water beneath the Palais Garnier – deep and vast enough for the Paris fire brigade to use it for practice rescue dives, tall enough such that regular inspections of the ceiling are conducted by small boat. However, the lake of the opera is not a lake at all but a concrete basin with a vaulted ceiling – rather like an indoor swimming pool. To those who know the truth behind the legend it is *"la cuve voûtée"* (the arched tank). The floor directly above the basin supports the stalls for the animals used in productions.

Though Garnier put the water to good use in clever ways, geography was the primary reason for constructing a pool in the second-level basement of the opera, for the site selected for the opera was marshy and had an underground stream coursing through it. Rather than build up the land or re-channel what is believed to have been an ancient cut-off course of the Seine, Garnier concluded that the most efficient way to protect the structure from flooding was to leave the tributary where it was and to make water a part of the foundation. Garnier knew that if the foundation had remained a hollow shell, constant water pressure from the exterior would weaken it and water would eventually seep in. But by filling the very bottom of the structure with water, pressure from the outside would equal that on the inside, thereby protecting the building from a catastrophic flood or a foundation collapse.[5]

The basin was designed to fill naturally from the tributary but in fact, the water was originally pumped in from the Seine over an eight-month period. The water would serve two purposes. One, it would be used to extinguish theater fires – a frequent occurrence back then due to heat and light sources. Second, and most impressively, water from the pool would provide the ballast needed to raise and lower the stage, seven stories above the basin.

It's clear from all the sneaking around in *Phantom* that Leroux knew the opera house inside and out. At seventeen stories tall from the basement to the roof, much of it is a rabbit warren of dark rooms, trap doors and tunnel-like passageways – the perfect setting for a whodunit. More than likely, the idea to put a foggy lake under the opera occurred to Leroux after he saw Garnier's curious pool in the basement.

Another scene that could only be created by someone with insider knowledge is the one in which a chandelier comes crashing down onto the orchestra section, killing several theater-goers and injuring many. The phantom takes in the pandemonium from up above, delighted that he has once again proven his point: he rules the house.[6]

The scene wasn't all imagination. The Palais Garnier does indeed have a magnificent eight-ton crystal chandelier suspended over the orchestra section. Though in reality only the stage moves up and down via hydraulic power from the basin, it is fun to speculate as to whether Leroux imagined his character invoking magic powers of the murky water below in order to execute his evil actions . . . like bringing down a chandelier.

Most intriguing is to contemplate the origin of Leroux's beguiling phantom named Erik – a grand mélange of a guy: tall, dark, handsome (well, at least in the acted versions), creepy, sensitive and very naughty. Added to that, he can carry a tune. What woman *wouldn't* fall for a guy like that?

During both the Franco-Prussian War (1870-71) and the brief Paris Commune (March to May 1871), several cellar rooms of the opera were used as prison cells. Rumor had it that passers-by at street level could hear the prisoners begging for their release, like poor beasts thrown into a dungeon and left to die. It would not require a huge stretch of the imagination for a writer to take this image and run with it, creating from it one of the most memorable and pitiful characters in modern-day drama.

Gaston confirms the use of the basement of the opera house as a prison in *Phantom*. Below, Raoul and the Persian piece together how the phantom was able to sneak around the opera house unseen:

> Later, he learned that Erik had found, all prepared for him, a secret passage, long known to himself alone and contrived at the time of the Paris Commune to allow the jailers to convey their prisoners straight to the dungeons that had been constructed for them in the cellars; for the Federates had occupied the opera-house immediately after the eighteenth of March . . . ."[7]

I got to see the watery basement of the opera house for myself one brilliantly blue and crisp day in September. After a twenty-minute reconnaissance mission around the sparkling Palais Garnier, I finally located the administrative entrance to the building, hidden behind a wrought iron gate and at the back of a parking lot. A security guard at the door accepted my one email message from Gilles Djéraouane, *Service Intérieur*, as proof enough of my importance, and waved me in. Once in, I sat in the lobby for twenty minutes, sharing one of two elegant wooden benches with six dancer types – both male and female. Svelte, beautiful and with the look of desperation on their faces, it was entirely plausible that these perfect specimens of the human race were waiting to audition for a part in a ballet.

When my turn came to explain myself, I produced the same email message that I had shown to the security guard. After reading the email message, the receptionist looked up again, this time eyeing me more closely. She took note of my scholarly-looking backpack/briefcase. Good sign. Then she told me to come back at 2:00 p.m.

"Mr. Djéraouane is not available at this moment," she announced. She left it at that.

Her response could have easily been interpreted as a brush-off. It wouldn't have been my first. But I kept the faith and returned three hours later at 2:00 p.m., right on the dot. To my amazement, upon my return the receptionist told me that Djéraouane was back and would see me now. She called him from her desk phone and a few minutes later a tall, dark and deliciously handsome man of Middle Eastern descent appeared before me. His smile made me weak at the knees – teeth as white and straight as piano keys, a surprisingly uncommon feature in France. The administrator's thick, dark hair was expertly feathered into the texture and shine of a crow's breast. With a sweep of his tanned and hirsute arm he directed me into his office. I eagerly followed him and as I did, I rehearsed in my head a two-minute recap of my project in French. Language skills would give me the edge that I needed, but I knew that charm would be the key to getting in.

The conversation began with an exchange of niceties: the usual chit-chat about the weather and how long I would be in Paris. The easy back-and-forth dialogue gave me a chance to warm up my French and to subtly flirt, a prerequisite to getting information out of any Frenchman. It worked. After my brief, to-the-point explanation of my project in perfect French amid a lot of smiling and feminine gesturing, Djéraouane told me to wait while he called down to the fire station, the one that resides right within the opera house. After explaining my mission to his colleague he nodded, said "*Merci*," and hung up the phone.

"Two firemen will meet us in the basement now," he said.

I was in!

It is extremely rare for an outsider to be shown the basin. None of the cataphiles whom I had interviewed had ever seen it. And afterwards, when I told my friend Artie, a nearly lifelong resident of Paris, that I had seen the basin she exclaimed, "You got to see the basin? *Nobody* in Paris ever gets to see basin!"

"I know," I said looking down, trying hard to suppress a smirk. "I don't know why he took me down." Then I responded coyly. "Maybe it was my accent."

Artie narrowed her eyes and glared at me.

"Maybe I should stop talking," I said, eyes lowered to feign apology.

To this day, I don't know why, after only one letter and an unannounced visit, Djéraouane warmly welcomed me into the inner workings of the opera house. But he did, and I am immensely grateful for his hospitality and generosity. After much reflection I've come up with three simpleton explanations as to why it happened. One, I was at the right place at the right time. Two, my French is very good and three, I have a highly developed skill for flirting. This had been one of those rare occurrences in my life when fate, skill and experience had come together in a good way (for once!) to land me exactly where I wanted to be. I could try to think up more explanations, but enough. Why look a gift horse in the mouth?

Back to the opera house. After he hung up the phone Djéraouane stood up and motioned for me to come with him. We didn't walk for very long before we passed through a door that led to a stairway made of plain metal rungs. As I followed him down one flight of stairs after another, the feeling was slightly reminiscent of my underground tour with the cataphiles. For a moment I wondered just how far down we were going.

In *Phantom* the "lake" is accessible through a wrought iron gate on rue Scribe, near the administrative entrance, and also through a trap door in one of the cellars. In the book Raoul and the Persian discover the phantom's secret route by pushing through the mirror in Christine's dressing room. I had wished for a more dramatic entrance to the basin but the stairs were but another instance where fiction and reality diverged.

When we reached the bottom, two levels below from where we had started, the air felt warm and humid and it smelled faintly like the Paris sewers. The two firemen, Apban Frantz and Eric Chaput, were already waiting for us when we arrived at the lowest level of the opera house, two floors below ground level. After Djéraouane introduced us, I gave the firemen a five-sentence overview of my project. Then, before he disappeared up the stairs Djéraouane flashed that gorgeous smile again and invited me to stop by his office after the tour, should I have any other questions. I had already decided that I would stop by on my way out, just to take in that 100-watt smile one more time.

After the dashing Djéraouane had cleared the stairwell and the three of us stood looking at each other, I decided that it was now or never. I just had to ask the fish question. Yes, FISH.

So I moved in close to my two guides, and with a subtle smile and a soft voice (works well with Frenchmen), I whispered in French, "I have heard that there are fish living in the basin. Tell me. Is this true?"

"*Oui, oui!*" they both answered in unison, broad grins flooding the place. They were eager to show and tell.

"Wait here," Chaput ordered. Then, like Djéraouane, he too bounded up the stairs and disappeared. A few minutes later he returned carrying half a baguette.

"Here," he said. "This will be our bait."

The sight of Chaput with a baton of bread tucked under his arm like architectural drawings made me giddy with excitement. Not only had I managed to talk my way into the basement of the Palais Garnier – one of the most famous buildings in the world – I was going to feed the fish living under it! Could my career in nonfiction writing get any better than this?

Accepting the baguette from Chaput I concluded that no, it couldn't. Standing in the basement of the Palais Garnier, posed to feed fish from the same spot that Gaston Leroux likely once stood and with two cute French firemen looking on had been the coolest thing I had ever done in the line of duty. But wait a minute. Hadn't I already said that about my illegal descent to subterranean Paris with the cataphiles? There was that, too.

Back to the "lake." Thus equipped with a baguette in one hand and a flashlight in the other, I followed Frantz and Chaput through a narrow, concrete corridor that led to a large open area. About forty feet away from where we stood, Frantz pointed to a square hole in the floor with metal rung stairs leading down.

"There," he motioned with his flashlight. "That is the basin."

I walked to the square opening and crouched down. I asked if I could climb down the ladder to see the basin better.

"Sure, go ahead," Frantz answered.

I'm sure that he and Chaput got a kick out of watching the American writer get so excited about what was to them, just a pool of icky water. While the men chatted I decided to take advantage of their distraction and climb down to the fourth rung, the last one above the water. Then, holding onto a rung with one hand, I reached down with the other and placed my outstretched palm flat onto the surface of the water. The two men saw my precarious balancing act but said nothing.

The water was frigid to the touch, a constant 50°F they told me. Then I crouched down as low as I could get, stretching even closer to the water so that I could shine a beam of light across the surface of the pool.

"Wow," I said out loud.

The author ascending from the "lake of the Opera." At least three species of fish live in the pool underneath the Palais Garnier. Photo by Apban Frantz

The basin is enormous in area: 121 feet in length by 171 feet in width.[8] With a uniform depth of about ten feet, it holds more water than an Olympic-sized swimming pool. I panned the light around the basin though I couldn't see all of it because the arches blocked full view of the pool. The 14-foot-high vaulted ceiling was as elegant as an ancient Roman bath. An oily residue and small debris floated on the surface. When I shone the light straight down into the water, I could see that the water column had suspended particles in it and that the floor of the basin was covered in a layer of silt. As an experienced scuba diver I knew that fine silt like this gets kicked up into clouds that disorient. In an underwater sandstorm you can't tell up from down. Untrained or inexperienced divers can panic and drown.

After I got a grasp of the area and shape of the pool, I handed back the flashlight and reached for the baguette, breaking off a few crumbs. While still perched on the last rung and with one of the men holding the light directly over the water, I sprinkled a few morsels into the water. Within thirty seconds of the white flecks hitting the murky water, the black silhouette of creatures one to two feet long appeared, darting here and there for the crumbs. Like a kid who has caught her first fish, I screeched with delight. The firemen told me that the feeding frenzy was that of catfish and barbel, both ancient, whiskered species with pointy snouts. From overhead they looked like miniature sharks. The largest might have weighed as much as seven pounds. Frantz told me that eels live in the basin too. As I perched on the rung ladder wearing on my feet nothing more than strappy black sandals (Italian, no less), my candy-apple red toenails just inches from the water, I was happy not to see any of these serpent-like *anguilliformes* vying for my bread crumbs.

Since the basin has been filled with city water for at least a century the obvious question is, how did the fish get there? According to the firemen, a sneaky opera house employee stocked the basin many years ago. The fish have thrived there ever since, living on other small creatures such as snails and algae. I didn't ask how *they* got there.

What with the possibility of horses just overhead in the stalls, a phantom still wandering loose in the imagination and now very real fish circling at my feet, I couldn't help but mutter with a giggle, "This place is a real zoo!" Of course my American humor was lost on the kind *pompiers* (firemen) but in this case, the expression truly fit.

The basin is a living antique, rich in history, culture and maybe even biology. Even so, I concluded that although it would make for a good story, under no circumstance did I want to tumble into this strange, cold brew. As a licensed diver I have even swum with small sharks in the area, but the thought of scuba diving in an enclosed, dark space and sharing it with the catfish, the eels and whatever other creatures the firemen didn't tell me about would be way too creepy.

Dangerous, too.

Although it isn't deep, exploring the basin is every bit as risky as cave diving for like a cave, the basin has no natural light. Added to that, the water is turbid, dangerously cold and there are columns to disorient. In a French-made documentary one professional diver says, "You can get lost in a moment . . . . An adventurous colleague can easily get lost and we must search for him in the maze of columns, snaking around them to find him."[9]

Nevertheless, in the opinion of a French rescue diver, diving in the basin of the opera is indeed a privilege. I can't blame him for feeling that way. After all, under how many world-class, fabulously elegant theaters can you scuba dive around Roman arches and come face-to-face with a seven-pound fish?

When I finally emerged from the bowels of this magnificent landmark and into the daylight, so great was the contrast between light and dark that I cowered from the blinding sun. Instinctively, I whipped away from the glare, shading my eyes and as I did, I recognized my own gesture: it was that of Leroux's phantom, the villain-victim who shunned the light of day and all of its nosy inhabitants. A part of me wanted to retreat back to the calm, the coolness and the privacy of the basement of the opera house. For a moment, I too had been transformed into a character of the imagination by the deepest, darkest secret of the Palais Garnier.

The lost Bièvre

Centuries ago the area in Paris that is now the 5th and 13th arrondissements was rural and poor. However, it had two advantages: wind and water. A meandering brook called the Bièvre once coursed through this hilly part of Paris. So that its hydraulic power could be tapped as it descended into the city, section by section engineers began converting the Bièvre into a canal of locks and dams.[10]

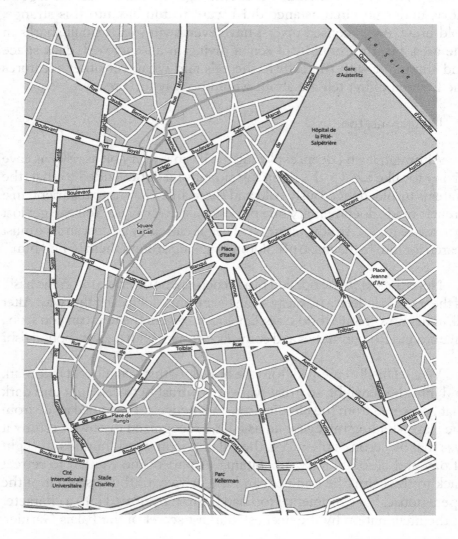

Route of the Bièvre River, a stream that once flowed through the Left Bank of Paris. Centuries of pollution and development have all but obliterated the Bièvre so that today it exists only as an underground pipeline. Map © Jean-François Ségard/ www.planete-echo.net/

Ever since Gallo-Roman times the Bièvre had served the city well, providing energy, water and even protection for the Latin Quarter from potential invaders. But as Paris grew, the banks of the Bièvre eventually became completely industrialized. Raw sewage, dyes from a tapestry-making complex, run-off from slaughterhouses and fishmongers, and discharge from paper mills and tanneries all ended up in the Bièvre. By the nineteenth century the stream-turned-canal was so polluted that it had become an odor nuisance. Worse yet, it threatened public health. Ecologically, the Bièvre was dead.

The response by officials was not to stop the pollution – well, eventually they did – but for the time being, to just cover it up. Work began in 1826 with projects that rerouted the canal under several boulevards. By 1910 the Bièvre was completely paved over, its flow rerouted to a collector sewer.

What's left today of the Bièvre within the city limits is an alley-like gutter deep below the street. Nevertheless, and in spite of centuries of human intervention that has all but obliterated the Bièvre, the stream still retains one unique function: it is the geological divide that separates the largest underground quarry, the *GRS* under the 14th arrondissement, from the lesser four under the 13th, 16th and 12th arrondissements.

In 2000 historians and environmentalists banded together to lobby for restoration of Paris' other river, calling themselves the "Union of Associations for the Renaissance of the Bièvre." Despite these efforts however, the Bièvre is nowhere in sight . . . at least not in Paris. None of the cataphiles whom I interviewed had seen the Bièvre, nor do they know where to find it – quite surprising given their extensive knowledge of the underground.

I tracked down what I thought was the Bièvre Historical Society one raw, rainy day in January – the kind of day that Paris travel agents try to keep under wraps. The address I had was 30 rue du Cardinal-Lemoine, in the heart of the Latin Quarter. I went there hoping I might find some sign of the Bièvre. Even if it were but an iron grate down into which I could have peered and caught a glimmer of water, I would have felt successful. But all that I saw that day at the busy intersection of rue du Cardinal-Lemoine and rue des Écoles was a post office, an Arab library and lucky for me, at least one cozy café to duck into for a pot of hot tea.

The funny thing is, as I sat in the café, gazing out at the dreary streetscape before me, though I didn't know it at the time, I was looking right at a Bièvre historic site – well, sort of. It wasn't until many months later that I put the pieces of this puzzle together. I had stumbled upon 30 rue du Cardinal-Lemoine because it was the address given on a website for an *"Agence de la Bièvre"* (Bièvre Agency). At the time however, I had no reason to associate a post office with the Bièvre River because the building has no signs, not even a plaque, to indicate that it houses a landmark related to the Bièvre. As it turns out, it does indeed.

Out of sight but not out of mind

So where does post office meet lost river? At an ancient wall. France's King Philippe-Auguste, not known for his acts of kindness but for his many acts of construction including Notre Dame Cathedral and Les Halles central marketplace, had also built a wall of defense around the city. Around 1167 the wall was altered to provide the monks living at St. Victor Abbey access to the Bièvre.

It was during renovation of 30 rue du Cardinal-Lemoine to make the ground floor of the building into a post office that workers discovered an ancient arch. Historians dated the stone structure to the twelfth century, concluding that it was a remnant of the Philippe-Auguste wall, specifically, the section that once spanned the Bièvre.

This ancient stone arch once spanned the Bièvre River. Photo by François Benveniste

In 1991 renovation of the arch was completed and it was such a big deal that the French government commissioned several artists to draw renderings of the arch, calling the exhibit, "The Adventures of the Lost Arch of the Bièvre." Five different interpretations were reproduced and sold as postage stamps and posters to commemorate the discovery.

Though the Bièvre may be out of sight, it is clearly not out of mind. Several efforts are under way in Paris suburbs to restore the Bièvre, and at least one travel agency advertises bicycle tours of the Bièvre Valley; hard to imagine when there is no sign of the river within city limits. However, the fact that someone can sell historic bicycle tours of the Bièvre Valley and that an artifact of a river last seen almost a century ago was the subject of an exhibit seems proof positive that this ancient stream holds significance in the French psyche.

Canal Saint-Martin

As part of his grand waterworks to rid Paris of water borne scourges once and for all, Napoléon III built three connected canals: the Ourcq, Saint-Denis and Saint-Martin, in order to bring cleaner water into the city from the hinterlands.[11] The smallest of them, canal Saint-Martin, funneled water right into the heart of Paris. As the Ourcq and Saint-Denis canals still are today, canal Saint-Martin used to be uncovered for its entire length. But as the city's needs changed, so too did the canal. While the wider Ourcq and Saint-Denis have remained uncovered for larger-scale navigation, the bed of the narrow Saint-Martin was lowered and about one third of it was covered over, converting it into a partially submerged waterway.

Since its alteration, the primary use of canal Saint-Martin has been recreational . . . and residential. Though you can't tell from a map, the canal actually starts at a basin called Port de Plaisance,[12] adjacent to the Bastille memorial. Tour boats set off from the basin and ply the canal all the way up to Port de la Villette in the 19th arrondissement all year round. What makes this Paris waterway so unique are the quaint houseboats moored in the basin and the canal's leafy, tree-lined banks – part Amsterdam, part yacht club – right in the middle of the city. If ever there were a competition for the most beautiful and convenient place to live in Paris, surely the Bassin Arsenal would be in the running. The best view of this picturesque water feature is from the Bastille Métro station, part of which perches directly over the basin.

A covered section of Canal Saint-Martin. Photo by Stéphane Mezei

Houseboats moored at the head of Canal Saint-Martin, near the Bastille.
Photo by Luc Nueffer

Though partially underground, a boat cruise down canal Saint-Martin feels nothing like an underground quarry nor the Catacombs. Whereas the former two are definitely creepy and potentially scary, canal Saint Martin is magical. Holes cut into in the ceiling of the tunnel to let in light cast perfectly round spheres of light onto the water. Rays of sun that filter through the grates above dance on the walls of the canal like flames on a cave wall.

In the case of quarry diving, the fear of being trapped is particularly acute. But there is no quick way out of the other subterranean structures like the Catacombs or even the sewers, either. That archetypal fear of being trapped underground is enough to drive away those even slightly prone to claustrophobia. But in the case of the canal Saint-Martin claustrophobics need have no fear. You can always see light at the end of the tunnel.

Make a wish

In order to monitor the water level of the *nappe phréatique* or in some cases, as a means to draw water, wells were built within the quarries. In French these wells are called fountains but they don't have water bubbling out of them. Rather, they are round holes carved out of stone that reach the *nappe*. The most noted "fountains" are those that have spiral staircases leading down to the water. One of them, Fountain of the Capucins under the Hospital Cochin, is so structurally beautiful that it has been designated a historic monument.

Two other underground "fountains" are *Bain de Pieds* (foot bath) and Chartreuse Fountain, an odd, square-shaped form in a quarry that was the German army's main bunker during the Occupation. Though not underground, Lamartine Fountain is the last artesian well still in service in Paris. You can get a taste of real eau de Paris from this drinking fountain located in the 16th arrondissement where avenue Victor-Hugo meets the Arc de Triomphe.

To the non-cataphile, these underground fountains are a curious thing. Since so few people ever get to see them, why bother to build them with such artistry? In fact, one could ask the same question about any of the art forms found all over subterranean Paris: the drawings, paintings, carvings, poetic messages and graffiti. Why take the time and energy to create something that will never see the light of day? I can't answer for a Frenchman but it seems to me that only a culture that regards the underground as a worthy destination in and of itself, would bother to put art there in the first place.

Bain de Pieds *(foot bath) underground "fountain."* Photo by Stéphane Mezei

A friend who lives in Paris once remarked, "The Paris sewers are full of hair dye." She was referring to the excess of unnatural blonds and redheads in Paris, especially among those of a certain age. I get her point. In Paris, hair dye must flow out of brown plastic bottles as abundantly as wine flows out of green glass ones. Just like Americans, Parisians chase after youth with equal vigor, employing all possible means to fool the clock. (I'll note that the French are beating Americans by a landslide on the race to stay thin.) But since nobody is pushing and shoving their way down the nearest manhole to fill up their bottles with water from the *nappe phréatique*, I'm confident that none of the fountains under Paris are the Fountain of Youth. So if you are lucky enough to see one of them, you will likely be quite alone.

But if you hang around long enough, who knows? You might spy a certain phantom making a wish.

Notes

1   The origin of the word "artesian" is *Arteis*, which was later called Artois, a former province in northern France, roughly equivalent to the present-day department of Pas-de-Calais. Artois had a spring whose water flowed to the surface naturally.

2   Paris water comes from three sources: natural springs tapped from rural sites outside of the city, and the Seine and Marne Rivers.

3   Paris has three manmade canals: Saint-Martin, Saint-Denis and the Ourcq.

4   Gaston Leroux, *The Phantom of the Opera: the original novel* (Buccaneer Books: New York, 1977), 264-265.

5   Marlene Justsen, Paul Mellon Research Fellow at the National Gallery of Art Archives, e-mail message to author, November 21, 2005. The East Building of the National Gallery of Art in Washington, D.C. was also built on a wetland. Like the Palais Garnier, a tributary once flowed through the site, its course following the present-day Constitution Avenue. In the case of the American museum however, architect I.M. Pei had a different solution. After pumping away ground water before and during construction, his plan called for a six-foot thick mat to be anchored thirty-seven feet below the surface. The giant waterproof mat made the foundation resistant to water pressure from the former Tiber Creek.

6   Note that in the book, Erik denies causing the chandelier to fall, claiming that it was old and worn and came loose on its own.

7   Leroux, *Phantom of the Opera*, 243-244.

8   Gilles Djéraouane, e-mail message to author, March 13, 2007, in which measurements were provided in metric form: 3.10m in depth, 37m length and 52m wide. The ceiling height under each arch is 4.20m.

9   Françoise Marie, *France: Beneath Paris* (Derry, New Hampshire: Chip Taylor Communications, 1998).

10   The mouth of the Bièvre was once near its namesake rue de la Bièvre in the 5th arrondissement, but it was subsequently rerouted so that it met the Seine near Austerlitz train station. What's left of the stream today is funneled into a wastewater pipeline.

11   Actually, the project began as one canal, the Ourcq. It was subsequently extended on both ends with Saint-Denis canal on one end and Saint-Martin canal on the other.

12   Its official name is *Port de Plaisance de Paris Arsenal* but Parisians refer to it as the *Bassin Arsenal* (Arsenal Basin).

Chapter 4

Hitting the Mall Under Les Halles

In the 1985 French film *Subway* the chase goes underground where schizophrenic Fred, a lovesick cat burglar and scam artist, takes refuge from henchmen and police. Down below in the Paris subway, Fred encounters a menagerie of misfits who dwell in this dark underworld, rarely venturing into society or sunlight. Whether for money, love or secret papers, someone is always after something. Eventually we learn of Fred's real dream: to assemble his own rock band and to draw unhappily married Héléne into his life on the edge.

What makes *Subway* unique is that the props and scenery are Parisian subway infrastructure and an underground shopping center. A purse snatcher on roller skates makes an Evel Knievel getaway down a station escalator. Fred follows the purse snatcher into a boiler room and then the grid floor drops out from under him. There is a squadron of dimwit policemen who manage to bungle every pursuit. The flower vendor is easily bribed with money or whiskey to snitch on his fellow outcasts.

Director Luc Besson may have had poor taste in music, but he knew a good movie set when he saw one. Almost the entire movie was filmed under Forum des Halles, a multi-leveled shopping/community/fitness complex that was planted, like an exotic invasive species, in the center of Paris. Two levels of a combined Métro/RER station called Châtelet are at the root of the complex. Within this station five hundred thousand people a day transfer trains, making it Europe's busiest. Besson used pipes, giant exhaust fans, long ladders, dark tunnels and moving walkways to create an oversized board game for his rejects. Though they may be screwed up, they roam their sunless territory free and accepted.

Forum des Halles can be deceiving at ground level, for less than half of the surface area is visible from the street. The entire complex plus the subway station stretches north from the banks of the Seine River at Île-de-la-Cité, all the way to rue Étienne Marcel, which borders on the 2nd arrondissement. Like the gate entrances to the once-walled medieval Paris, the three street side entrances to Les Halles are referred to as *ports* (doors). The underground passageways are so numerous that planners gave them the same trademark blue street signs seen throughout Paris and call them *rues* (streets). A *place* is where they intersect. So, for example, if you ask for directions to the swimming pool, you'll be told to enter Les Halles at the Porte du Jour and proceed to the Place de la Rotonde.

Eight hundred years of shopping

Nearby churches Saint-Eustache and Saint-Germain-l'Auxerrois were the site of the city's first market square. In 1183, the same year that construction began on the venerable Notre Dame Cathedral, King Philippe Auguste enlarged the square and built a shelter for merchants who came from all over France to sell their produce and wares. Philippe Auguste's plan worked for the first 779 years, but when automobiles and a lot more people moved into Paris, operating a wholesale food market in the middle of a metropolis of seven million people (now nearly ten million including suburbs) became cumbersome, to say the least. Furthermore, transportation planners were preparing to build an RER station under Les Halls to connect with the Châtelet Métro station already there. For these reasons, in 1962 the market with ancient roots was moved out to a site near Orly Airport.

Residents strongly opposed the move and were loathe to see officials tinker with Paris ground zero. Indeed, their concerns were warranted, for once the digging commenced in 1971, Les Halles became known as *le trou* (the hole), and it wasn't filled in completely until the end of the eighties. During that time at least ten architects made proposals for the site. One such was to make Les Halles into a yacht harbor by filling in the hole with water and building a canal to connect it to the Seine. You can imagine what the other nine were like.

Eventually what got built was the vast Forum des Halles, a place where shopping could continue for maybe another eight hundred years. This was, quite literally, what urban planners call "infill development," the opposite of sprawl. The middle of the complex was left as an open plaza so that from the air Les Halles might resemble an upside down Egyptian pyramid with giant steps leading downward. The genius of an open middle is that even three stories below buildings get natural light, camouflaging the fact that they are built into the ground . . . Leave it to the French to use space efficiently.

Above-ground portion of Forum des Halles. Photo by Valerie Broadwell

Les Halles includes, among other things, a multiplex cinema, an Olympic-sized swimming pool, a gymnasium, a carousel, shops, restaurants, a post office, a tropical plant atrium and underground parking. The complex descends more than one hundred feet into the ground, the equivalent of a ten-story building. Below the whole shebang are the Métro and RER stations, occupying two more levels below.

Operating Les Halles is comparable to running an airport terminal or Disneyland. Dozens of technicians, firemen and custodians work behind the scenes 24/7 to provide power, air, water, waste removal and security to a complex that draws one hundred thousand consumers, commuters, visitors and workers a day; 42 million a year.

Chain reaction

Although Les Halles is superbly designed – no mall in the U.S. even comes close to delivering so much style, diversity and efficient use of space – old timers say that the sense of community once associated with the 1st arrondissement has disappeared. Hardly any trace remains of the previous working-class neighborhood that centered around an open air pavilion flanked by local bars and bistros. Sadly, like so many American urban cores, Les Halles has had a chain reaction. Starbucks, Pier I Imports, The Gap, Claire's Boutique, FNAC (a French department store) and McDonald's all occupy space there, sucking up business from the locally owned shops surrounding Les Halles.

In addition to the economic havoc that Les Halles has wreaked on surrounding merchants, the exterior of the complex has a seedy feel, like that of a tired strip mall from the seventies. Litter and some gang activity at the street entrances make the place intimidating and cold. But the real crime is that a gargantuan structure loaded with chain stores was plunked down smack dab in the heart of Paris.

Generally, Parisians don't mince words when asked for an opinion, and railing against Les Halles was no exception. Speaking her mind, one passerby who lives not far away in the 2nd arrondissement snipped, "The real damage to Les Halles was the extension of the RER B line to the north, bringing all sorts of lowlife into the center of the city. People dislike this place because of the riff-raff hanging around, mainly kids from the dingier suburbs."

Scanning the crowd nervously, the attractive middle-aged woman added, "High levels of pickpocketing and loitering."

Architecturally, the complex doesn't quite fit in, though clearly an attempt was made. The structure's glass and metal roof is reminiscent of Hector Guimard's famous Art Deco Métro entrances, but it sprouts up amid nineteenth century building rooftops, and poses an incongruous silhouette against the stately Notre Dame Cathedral, just in the backdrop. No wonder locals don't like the place.

Miss Personality Plus

Even with a map, it took me a good hour to find the administrative offices of Les Halles and no wonder, the place covers fourteen acres in area. The colorful reception area, set behind imposing double glass doors, was smartly decorated with primary colors and clean lines. When I came in nobody was behind the white enamel receptionist's desk, so I waited. I figured the place was probably staked out with hidden cameras; someone had to know I was there. Sure enough, about three minutes later an overly thin, overly blond young woman wearing retro, thickly framed glasses appeared from nowhere. Her skin was so pale that she could have been a ghost. After issuing the requisite "*Bonjour Madame*" greeting, she asked if she could help me.

In flawless French I asked if I might be able to spend a few minutes talking to the operations chief for a book I was writing on subterranean Paris. As I spoke, she gave me that uniquely Parisian, uncompromising smirk of the lowly bureaucrat who is delighted to be in the power seat. Before I could even finish describing my project she cut in, "No, no. That is not possible, Madame." She then flung a glossy brochure onto the countertop that separated me from her and began writing.

"All of the information on Les Halles is at this website," she said, scribbling down a URL. "If you have further questions after you've looked at the website, you may write a letter to this address here," she told me, pointing to an address on the brochure.

I stopped talking, smiled ever-so-slightly and stared down at the brochure along with her. The strange thing however, was that as I watched her write, my attention was drawn not to the four-color brochure but to the woman's long, red fingernails that matched perfectly her shiny, blood-red lips. The thought occurred to me that rather than looking chic, as she had intended, she looked as if she had just killed and eaten someone or something – a small child or perhaps a French poodle. I pictured the frail, blond thing crouched in the back room, gorging on her kill, face first. How dare I disturb the feast!

Though she took me for a stupid tourist, I had already sized her up as an arrogant bureaucrat. A website wasn't going to do, or, as the French say, *Ça ne va pas aller* ("This isn't going to work"). I had come a long way from home; scurried through ancient subterranean tunnels; felt the cold, murky water of the phantom's lake; talked my way into the Métro central command center. This haughty little woman who could have quite possibly been a cannibal or an apparition, was not going to scuttle my plans. So I moved to plan B: I coldly bid Miss Personality Plus a thank you and a good bye, turned on my heels and set about on my own course of exploration.

Shark feeding frenzy

On this raw and wet January day plan B was to find an activity underground that would be fun, relieve stress and not involve shopping . . . my personal version of hell on earth. Surely within the halls of Les Halles I would find something.

Since I hadn't gone through the bureaucratic channels first, I knew that the chances of getting an on-the-spot interview with the chief of operations or even one of the engineers was unlikely, so I came prepared for other adventures. I had packed swim gear, exercise clothes, my laptop, a tape recorder and a camera. This left me lots of options for trying out the facilities or the people, whatever and wherever they may be.

As a once-dedicated lap swimmer, the pool was the first place that came to mind. It was morning and I had all day to find it, if that's what it took. After a half-mile lap swim me and my laptop would settle into a cozy café, one of dozens in Les Halles. Maybe I would even try the Starbucks.

So, after a thirty-minute reconnaissance mission to find one Olympic-sized pool, I finally found the *Piscine des Halles* (Halles Pool) in the Suzanne Berlioux Sports Center, Level-3. Although the pool is below ground, one side is all glass and it actually functions as the fourth side of a tropical plant atrium situated on the outdoor plaza. The plants and trees give the pool a warm, sunny feel – unexpected in a place three stories below the surface. The pool had about six lap lanes open, all with at least five swimmers per lane. Ouch . . . crowded. I picked a lane with medium-fast swimmers and hopped in. When there was enough space between myself and the swimmer in front of me, I ducked under the water, kicked off the side and swam for almost half the length of the pool before coming up for air. While underwater I listened hard for the sound of subway trains below, lumbering into the Châtelet station. But I heard only the muted splashing of the other swimmers. There was no perceptible vibration, either. When I came up for air I started to free stroke and I felt free and at peace. This was exactly where I wanted to be.

But the peace would not last for long.

I was moving at a good clip when a swimmer came up fast from behind and slapped me on the foot. I figured it must have been an accident. Maybe without his contacts in the guy was blind as a bat. When he passed me mid-lane he made such a wake that I took in water and started to cough.

"Okay, so he's a blind *whale*," I thought to myself.

A few minutes later another swimmer did the same thing. Then another. This was no accident. Was a slap on the foot how French swimmers signaled they were going to pass? Were they trying to tell me to move out of the fast lane? (None of the lanes were marked.) All of these theories were plausible except for the fact that after the swimmers passed me I would arrive at the end of the lane only to find them standing there, panting. Either the Gauloises cigarettes had gotten to them or they didn't know how to pace themselves. In either case, these guys in their skimpy Speedos weren't athletes.

I, on the other hand, was accustomed to the orderly, graceful ways of serious lap swimmers in the States. The mark of a good swimmer is one who cuts through the water like a dolphin, hardly making a splash. The expert lap swimmer maintains a courteous distance between him and the swimmers ahead. In order to avoid collisions, passing usually occurs at the end of the lane, not mid-way. But this pool had so much slapping, flapping and passing going on that I felt like I was slogging through a monsoon.

Another thought that came to mind was that the other swimmers were trying to hit on me. Maybe this is how Parisian guys made pool pick-ups, by harassing their prey in the water so they became tired out. Then, while "resting" at the side, they would attempt conversation. Good grief.

As my nerves became undone from what should have been a relaxing activity, it occurred to me that the problem was not pool etiquette, but driving etiquette. These guys tailgated then passed, cut me off, suddenly braked mid-lane and occasionally yelled at other swimmers. Where had I seen that before? Driver's Ed had taught me how to drive defensively. I never thought I would need to apply those skills in a pool. But for Parisians, lap swimming and driving share the same ground rules. I suppose I could have tried dodging the other swimmers, yielding to them at the end of each lap, sticking close to the rope. But that was too much work. Besides, I wouldn't be able to maintain a constant pace, which, after all, is the whole point of aerobic exercise.

I never did figure out French pool etiquette before leaving, but one final theory I had was that the harassment was male chauvinism, since I was the only female in a lap lane. There were other women in the pool at the time but they were daintily paddling around the open swim area á la Esther Williams. Maybe the guys just didn't like having a female swimmer keep up with them or worse yet, swim faster than them.

Hula hoop drill sergeant

After having swum about a quarter of a mile, I decided that the stress of trying to swim laps in a pool that had more testosterone than chlorine wasn't worth it. If I wanted high anxiety all I needed to do was rent a car and drive around the Arc du Triomphe a few times. So I got out, changed into my exercise clothes, dried my hair and continued on my journey. What next? Surely, in a complex the size of eight football fields I could find something else to do.

The solution was right under my nose. When I exited the locker room I looked straight ahead and down, through a glass observatory, into a huge gymnasium. At one end there was a volleyball game going on; in the middle, a girls' gymnastics class and at the far end, about a dozen teenaged girls learning how to hula hoop . . . . Hula hoop? Who would have ever expected to see hula hooping in the center of Paris? Yet, here it was.

As I spied on the class from above, watching the teenaged girls giggle and fidget with their hoops, I had a flashback to age nine in the alley behind the house that I grew up in, circa 1969. I had outlasted everyone else in my neighborhood and was voted hula hoop champion of the alley kids. It was at that moment that I knew I had to do this. Not only would hula hoop be easy for me, I could be the star!

It is with these thoughts of grandeur that I skipped down the flight of stairs that separated me from the sports center information desk and boldly walked where no other forty-something American woman had gone before: into a French hula hoop class. Was the class open to the public? Yes. Could I join now? Yes. There was still space. When did the class start? About fifteen minutes ago. Perfect!

When I strutted in the instructor nodded to me and said "*Bonjour.*" She told me her name was "Crystale" (not her real name). I introduced myself and apologized for being late. Crystale pointed to a box of hula hoops and I picked one out, the candy striped variety. Then the instructor walked over to the blaring boom box and turned down the exotic belly dancing music.

"Listen everybody," she ordered in French.

Silence.

Already I could tell that Crystale was way too serious considering she was teaching people how to use a product made by Wham-O. Like the receptionist in the administration office, Crystale was also a bleached blond, only she was letting her dark roots grow out, so she had more color. Her eyebrows were plucked too thinly though, and she had the deep, raspy voice of a smoker. Smoking, and maybe the hula hooping, were probably what kept her so thin. Though she looked taut and in shape, she struck me as a woman who was trying too hard to be beautiful. Still, I respected her for taking her job so seriously. She was no pushover.

Several of the girls rattled their hoops, anxious to jig.

"Do NOT begin until I say," she barked. Crystale then explained that hula hoops work when the hips maintain enough centrifugal force to overcome gravity. If the hips don't do their job, the hula hoop falls.

Thanks for the news flash.

Next, our instructor turned her back to the class and gave us a demo. She was good, all right. The French have a knack for doing everything with more style and grace than anyone else in the world, and Crystale did not disappoint. She could have kept that hula hoop going for years. Her narrow hips swung in perfect little circles, feet planted firmly on the ground, not too close together but close enough so that she looked like a modern-day ballerina in bell-bottomed leggings and a clingy, paprika-orange midriff top.

The class watched in wonder and admiration, nobody making a move. It was almost hypnotizing. But the silence was soon broken when the girl in front of me sneezed and her hoop slipped out of her grasp. It hit the shiny gym floor with a CRACK, magnified several decibels by gymnasium acoustics. The poor nymph jumped and Crystale whirled around like a gladiator, ready for battle. She glared at the girl, who sheepishly picked up her hoop and stood still as a statue, mortified.

This lesson was becoming both comical and boring – but I reminded myself that at least it wasn't a war of the sexes in ten feet of water. Still, I was anxious to do rather than listen. Although I've spent many years struggling to become fluent in French, I've never forgotten the one advantage to being a non-native speaker of the local language: you can always feign ignorance. I therefore decided I would hasten Crystale's lecture by giving my hula hoop a whirl despite her orders. Looking straight at my instructor, I smiled and gave my hula hoop an exuberant spin.

She froze in shock at such defiance. Her mouth dropped, nose flared. All eyes turned on me. I struggled to keep the hoop afloat, my body contorting this way and that in a hopeless, pathetic attempt to prove my worthiness. But alas, thirty-five years of abstinence showed. Gravity won out and the hoop fell to my feet.

"Madame! Please, do not start until I tell you to!" yelled Crystale, her deep voice carrying throughout the gymnasium like an air raid alarm. Everybody in the gym, including the volleyball players at the opposite side of the gym, looked our way.

"I'm sorry," I said in French. "I did not understand."

I picked up my hoop but kept my eyes on the floor, hoping Crystale wouldn't see my grin. The girls on either side of me, daring to glance at the class clown, were relieved to see that my ego was still intact. When Crystale turned away from the class to give another demo, several more of my classmates made eye contact with me and rolled their eyes in commiseration. Everybody felt sorry for me but me. From my perspective, even if hooping proved to be boring, just watching this drill sergeant in action was a gas. Plus, something inside told me I could learn more from this woman than just hula hooping. She had a fire in her belly that intrigued me.

After one last demo and a few more paragraphs on the science of gravity, Crystale finally gave us the go ahead to try it for ourselves.

She cranked up the Arabic music and we all gave our hoops a whirl. The noise produced from twelve hoops continuously hitting the floor all but drowned out the music, but I wasn't listening anyway. I was thrilled to discover that after about five minutes of practice (and a side ache), my childhood talent returned. I got to the point where I could keep up my hoop up almost indefinitely. I was nine years old again!

Crystale saw me going to town and shouted, "Bravo!" She even smiled. My classmates clapped and I, class clown, was redeemed.

Eventually all but one or two of the girls got the hang of it. Crystale began to loosen up and she even showed us some tricks like hula hooping around the ankle and hula hoop throwing. She staged a contest to see who could last the longest. Not wanting to be too much of a show off I claimed that my side ached too much to compete. So along with Crystale I volunteered to be a judge rather than a contestant. I kept track of time as, one by one, the hoops fell to the floor until the new champion was left standing. She was elated.

As the fun side of Crystale emerged, my curiosity about her increased. She was around my age, attractive and, no doubt, a bit out of the ordinary to be a hula hoop instructor. I wondered what she did in her real life. Was she a teacher? A fitness instructor? Did she live near Les Halles? And most importantly, did those great abs come from hula hooping? (If so, it could be the next rage after Pilates.) Since it wasn't noon yet when the class ended I decided to ask Crystale if she wanted to have coffee with me. I told her that I was writing a book about Paris and that it included a chapter on Les Halles.

"Is the book about where one goes to exercise in Paris . . . when the weather is terrible?" she joked.

"No," I answered. "It's more of a travel book. But actually, a book on fitness opportunities in Paris is a great idea!" I told her. (It was in fact, a brilliant idea. I had already decided that my book would leave out lap swimming, though.)

Hula hoop lessons in the below-ground gymnasium of Les Halles. Photo by Valerie Broadwell

Crystale responded that she had forty-five minutes before her next class. Coffee would be great. I didn't ask but wondered, devilishly, whether Les Halles offered a whole series on American backyard fun. What would be next on the schedule . . . . Frisbee? Slip 'n Slide? Red Light, Green Light? I pictured model-thin, perfectly coiffed French women in spandex and low-cut T-shirts awkwardly trying to throw their Frisbees vertically. In another class they were sailing down a Slip 'n Slide at unsafe speeds then hitting the dry floor with a shock that sent them tumbling. The class after that? Trampoline!

In addition to housing the gym and pool entrances, Level-3 conveniently had a Starbucks, no doubt strategically sited there to capture exhausted Parisians streaming from the sports center, desperate for a cigarette. Going to the Starbucks was an easy decision since all we had to do was walk about one minute and we were there.

After we sat down with our coffee, I asked Crystale how she got into teaching hula hoop. She had a job as a part-time paralegal, a profession she had recently entered after completing a one-year course. Before that she did clerical work. Paralegal wasn't that different only the pay was a lot better. Since the law firm she worked for could only offer her a part-time schedule for the moment, she was making ends meet by teaching courses at the fitness center. As a school girl she liked dance and gymnastics, so teaching introductory classes like hula hoop or beginner yoga was easy. Then she lit up a cigarette.

Like so many French women, Crystale could have had four kids and you would have never known it from looking at her midriff. French people – both men and women – watch what they eat and what they wear much more closely than Americans. As it turns out, Crystale was a single mother of three. I wondered what she did to accomplish and maintain that perfectly flat stomach. Had she had a tummy tuck or liposuction? Was it hula hooping, yoga or good genes? I didn't have the courage to ask her but two Middle Eastern men sitting at the next table did have the courage to ask her if they could join us.

"No thank you," Crystale said, smiling. They were a sleazy twosome, that I could tell. Crystale was nicer than I would have been but then again, when you're in your forties and two twenty-something guys hit on you, it isn't all bad. This was her territory so I let Crystale handle it. Besides, warding off pick ups was not my strong suit.

The young men persisted. One of them came over to our table to ask whether we were waiting for someone. How lame a pick up line was that? Did we look "alone"? Furthermore, little did he know that he was playing with fire. Crystale was the pit bull of hula hoop instruction and I, 1969 neighborhood champ. Clearly, these bozos didn't know what they were getting into.

Our combined résumé sounded good in my head but it didn't play out well in conversation. After all, what could I have said to convey our power and skill? "Back off guys, our hips can MOVE!"

I kept my mouth shut. Observing Crystale's expertise at ridding us of bonehead was a study in first-rate bitchiness. Looking straight ahead she took a deep drag on her cigarette. Then she turned only her head toward him and slowly blew the smoke right into his face.

"*Tu t'es pas regardé,*" she stated, a classic French insult that translates roughly to, "Take a good look in the mirror, jackass." I took note of her use of *tu* (you) instead of the more respectful *vous*. Ouch. Further insult.

The guy stood there for a moment, transfixed, no doubt in shock at such confidence and . . . well . . . balls. But Crystale did not flinch. When it apparently hit him what had just happened he mumbled "*D'accord,*" ("Okay") and walked back to his table. I think at that point he was afraid of her.

"Wow, that was easy," I thought to myself.

It was obvious that the guy had been humiliated. When he went back to his table, tail between his legs, he kept a smirk on his face. After he sat down he quipped something to his buddy, then took a sip of his coffee. I tried not to look their way but like a rubber necker driving past a bad car accident, I had to see the carnage for myself. In this case the victim was trying to pretend that the whole thing had really been just a big joke.

Oh it was funny all right. But the joke was on him. Bravo, Crystale.

Nobody bothered us after that; word travels fast in a Parisian café. When it came time to leave I paid the bill and we walked down the mall together, more guys eyeing Crystale as we passed. She rattled off her weekly class schedule and invited me to come back for another class. I joked that I would come back for yoga only if she promised not to yell at me.

"I can't promise that," she teased, laughing at herself and the hothead image she projected. Yes, there was much to learn from this woman. I liked her.

We said good bye the way French friends do, with cheek kisses, and went our separate ways.

Lunch was my next stop. Most of the restaurants in Les Halles are located at street level so that they can draw customers from both the surrounding area and from the mall. I studied my map of Les Halles once again and decided to head for a large, sit-down café called *Flunch* (lunch + French?). The restaurant had an outdoor area on the plaza which would have been a good place to people watch, but the weather was so awful that eating outdoors was out of the question. So I found a table buried in a corner, far from drafts. From the self-service case I took a *salade Niçoise*, a lemon tart and a bottle of sparkling mineral water.

The place was packed, many patrons eating soup on this raw day – probably traditional French onion. But I was glad that I had ordered the salad. The potatoes were firm and full of flavor, the result of having marinated a good long time in spicy vinaigrette sauce. The green beans were cooked just right; bright green in color and not the least bit droopy. The anchovies were fresh tasting and oily, not dry and fishy as they are in the States. As do all dishes in France, a hunk of French bread came with the salad. It was crisp as toast on the outside, cottony soft on the inside; perfect for mopping up the vinaigrette dressing. The lone, sun-dried black olive on top of the salad, a delight.

To my side sat a well-groomed woman in her late fifties or early sixties, chowing down on what looked like half a chicken. Her hair was too red but even sitting, I could tell that she had the slim figure of a woman half her age. From the corner of my eye I watched as she ate everything on her plate then wiped the plate clean with bread. After a *crème brûlée* for dessert, she sipped an espresso while she smoked a cigarette, clearly satisfied. Spying on her reminded me of the difference in dining culture between the States and France. The French take the time to enjoy food; Americans only do so on special occasions. It has always been my theory that because our daily mealtimes are so socially unsatisfying, we never stop eating. America is a nation of obsessive snackers . . . and it shows.

I was tempted to hibernate in this warm, cozy spot for the rest of the afternoon, watching people enjoy their meals, tapping away on my laptop and sipping hot black tea English style, with sugar and milk. French restaurateurs never rush patrons in order to turn over more tables. As long as you've bought something, the space is yours for as along as you want it. I wanted it, but I had to move on. There were still people and places to see, things to do.

Serious people watching

My next stop was the Châtelet-Les Halles subway station. If you want to do some serious people watching in Paris, a subway station is the place to go, and Châtelet is the granddaddy of stations. If you're transferring there for the first time, be prepared to spend time piecing together your route. Even for me, a seasoned subway traveler, Châtelet feels like a dizzying amusement park only in this case the rides are connector tunnels, moving walkways, turnstiles and escalators. You might compare the dozens of shops, wall maps and directional signs to a fairground midway. Musicians, beggars, drunks, hunky police officers and enthusiastic lovers round out the scene.

At least half of the people who were bustling their way through the station had either a cell phone or MP3 player earphones glued to their heads. It is a miracle that there are not more collisions. When two people do collide, they always apologize to one another, but without lingering. Within seconds each has recovered and moved on, probably never to cross paths again.

Rush hour is the time to observe the subway at its finest. I am always amazed at how well it functions so that at the end of each day, every rider has gotten to his or her unique destination, no matter how far flung from the center city.

The pace is frenetic at Châtelet-Les Halles subway transfer point during rush hour. Photo by Valerie Broadwell

As a general rule but especially during rush hour, passengers move in and out of trains not as individuals, but as a unit. When I was a novice passenger I used to worry that I wouldn't make it out of a train or onto a packed train before the doors slammed shut. But I began to wonder whether my fears were unfounded after I observed that nobody ever got squished or trapped in a train at their stop. So one day I took a leap of faith: I let myself melt into the lava flow of humanity and it worked. It seems that as long as you remain part of the "glob," you will make it on and off trains, even at rush hour. Just trust and go with the flow.

At Châtelet I found a bench on a platform that had several sets of tracks on either side. As each train unloaded it produced a new tide of bodies that drifted past me like ragtag schools of fish. Luc Besson must have found his *Subway* characters by doing just as I was doing, sitting in a station and watching people. They were all there: the beautiful, bored trophy wife (played in the movie by Isabelle Adjani); the shady purse snatcher; the blind musician; Fred, the intense, burned out rocker; the obsessive drummer; the snitch with shifty eyes.

One giant sucking sound

A local merchant who sells souvenirs near Les Halles told me that it is really only the multiplex theater that brings people to Les Halles. In an effort to spruce up the place and appeal to bigger spenders, there is a plan to tear down Les Halles and rebuild it. "Les Halles II" would be better connected underground and it would contain mainly upscale clothing stores. Since the Châtelet-Les Halles subway station is over capacity at rush hour and nearing capacity even during off hours, it is conceivable that transportation planners will come up with a grand plan to extend the Météor or SNCF's Eole train to Châtelet, burrowing yet further down. Locals fear an even bigger, deeper *trou* (hole) is on the horizon. Maybe with one giant sucking sound, the next excavation will completely flush the entire 1st arrondissement down the proverbial toilet, along with any of its critics.

As the time got closer to rush hour, the activity level in the station became frenetic. Trains rumbled in and out continuously. Nobody remained seated on my bench for longer than a minute or two before getting up to board a train. I loved the anonymity of sitting there, invisible. In fact, I enjoyed it so much that I wondered whether I too was one of the misfits in *Subway*. After all, here I was, alone and content in this underworld. But when I thought about all the characters that I, like Fred, had encountered on my adventure: the nasty receptionist, a pod of aggressive male swimmers, two uncool guys looking for a pick up, one very cool hula hoop instructor and a saucy redhead who knew how to enjoy a meal, I arrived at the conclusion that this whole place was full of eccentric misfits – both good and bad – all chasing after something. Spend a day wandering around a place packed with this much humanity and you're bound to bump into a few of them.

At around seven o'clock in the evening the station crowd had noticeably thinned out. By this hour everyone was either preparing dinner or eating it. Those who weren't wished they were.

Even the gangs of roving policemen with sniffing dogs must have gone home to eat. According to a French friend, the police always patrol the subway in groups of seven to ten. When I asked why, he said that if the police aren't in a group, gangs jump them and their guns are stolen. It figures. *GQ* cops outfitted in shiny, black leather boots and peacock-blue jumpsuits that fit like a glove, but the fact remains: they're not that useful. Even the police dogs seem just for show. Their coats are immaculate but the only thing I've ever seen one sniff out was my travel companion's ham sandwich. And in that case the "contraband" was, well, right under the dog's nose.

What character am I?

I was certainly in the right place to find transportation home so I got up, finally, to find a subway wall map. My back was stiff and my butt sore from sitting on the hard bench and no wonder, I had been there for almost three hours! What great entertainment this was at so little cost. I knew I had to get to Gare du Nord in order to catch the RER C line back to a friend's apartment outside of Paris. As expected, it took me a good fifteen minutes to find the right platform. Had it still been rush hour, it would have taken me easily twice as long to get through the human traffic jam that forms daily at Châtelet.

When I found my lone Métro line one floor up, the platform was barren compared to the RER mega station from which I had just come. In less than five minutes a square, teal-green train rolled into the station and I boarded, wondering whether this time I was the one being watched. I wondered what character would I be in a screenplay about subterranean Paris . . . Quirky tourist? Chameleon? Dreamy American? Passionate, insightful writer? I would have liked the last.

I'll be back to Forum des Halles. Who knows what this eight-hundred-year-old marketplace will morph into? My only hope is that the next time around, city officials will have a plan in mind before tearing up the place. Maybe Les Halles II will be better, maybe not.

So be it. Les Halles goes on. As long as I can come back for "Advanced Hula Hoop" and find a great *salade Niçoise*, it's all good.

Chapter 5

Dem Bones

Across town from the heights of Montmartre and the Buttes-Chaumont, eighty feet below Place Denfert-Rochereau in the 14th arrondissement, rest the bones of nearly seven million Parisians whose skulls and bones are neatly stacked up like children's blocks. The sign at the main entrance says, "Stop! Here is the empire of the dead."

This warning proved useful to the French Resistance. Perhaps reasoning that the spirits were on their side, they literally went underground during the German Occupation, exploiting their insider knowledge of subterranean Paris to their advantage.

Late in World War II the *Forces Françaises de l'Intérieur* (French Forces of the Interior or *FFI*), built a full-service underground base called *abri FFI* (FFI shelter). On August 20, 1944, Colonel Henri Rol-Tanguy and his staff moved into the shelter so that he could direct an insurrection against the German Occupation. As it turned out, once the Allied Forces invaded at Normandy, the Germans cleared out of Paris *toute suite*, making the planned worker strikes and barricades unnecessary. Nevertheless, in August 2004, a tiny stretch of street near place Denfert-Rochereau was renamed after Rol-Tanguy, thereby changing the Catacombs' official address to 1, avenue du Colonel Henri Rol-Tanguy.

Among other amenities, *abri FFI* had its own power generator, toilets, dormitories, a medical suite and supplies of food and water – everything needed for a long stay. This shelter in particular, was prime real estate because it had connecting passageways to the sewers and to the subway – two other underground systems that the Resistance used for communication and for cover. The Resistance also selected this site because of its proximity to the phone center for all of Paris. With access to the city's central phone box, they cleverly wired the shelter so that the team could freely communicate with the outside by phone yet remain undetected by the Germans.

Legend has it that the ghosts of the Catacombs protected the Resistance. The Nazis, spooked by the thought of all those spirits lurking about, stayed away from the Catacombs and never discovered *abri FFI*.

As for the Nazis, though they stayed away from Denfert-Rochereau, they used the underground too, building several elaborate bunkers in ironically, the same quarry used by the Resistance, the *GRS* (Large Southern Network). But because the GRS is so vast, the two sides never bumped into one another . . . at least not underground, and Resistance fighters were able to spy for the Allied Forces as well as help coordinate attacks – all from the hidden underbelly of Paris.

Going back

The first time I saw the Paris Catacombs I was a 19-year-old college student. Over twenty years of my life had gone by before I went back. This time, I went down with my 19-year-old niece, Charisse. I was curious to see what her reactions to the Catacombs would be since she was now the same age that I had been when I first went down.

Going back much later in life I would learn that the Catacombs hadn't changed, but I had . . . . or so I thought. They still intrigued me as they had back then. Maybe it is because of the irony that I see there – that a place where death literally stares you in the face can also serve as a kitschy, if not curious, tourist attraction. For those who can overcome the skull and bones part, the "I'm-gonna-die-one-day" funk, the Catacombs are a place rich in history, tragedy, mystery . . . even spirituality.

My hope and hunch was that Charisse would be the type to overcome the creepiness of the place. Nevertheless, the thought of her freaking out after realizing that she was eighty feet down under with millions of dead people did cross my mind. This wasn't Charisse's first trip to Paris, but unlike any other tourist attraction she had been to, the Catacombs are wet, quiet and dark. You might find yourself alone quite often. And in addition to being deep underground, you are in close proximity to a lot of dead people – millions in fact. For Americans it is a foreign and eerie concept.

For this reason, I was mildly concerned that once Charisse got below the surface, panic might overtake her. Then, like a scene from a teen horror flick, she would break away and go tearing down one of the long, dark tunnels, screaming to get out. I would be running after her in hot pursuit, trying desperately to grab hold of her before she either tripped and fell into a catatonic state of fright or ran into a limestone wall head-first, knocking herself out cold.

I was scraping an imaginary Charisse off the muddy floor of the Catacombs when the real one called me back to the present. In her sing-song voice she chirped, "No Aunt Val, I won't freak out. I *really* want to go."

So I agreed to let her come, happy to have the company but wary that she might need to bail out . . . or rather up . . . at any given moment. Sometimes the Catacombs do that to people.

A place to put all of the dead

Little did I know that Charisse's reaction to the Catacombs would be way more entertaining than the intrigue of the Catacombs. During our Métro ride over to Place Denfert-Rochereau she asked me the obvious question, "Why did they put bones down there? I mean, why didn't they just bury the dead bodies like normal?"

The answer? Overcrowding. By the end of the 18th century, Paris cemeteries dating back to medieval times had become so full that they began to threaten public health. The largest of them, *Cimetière des Innocents* (Cemetery of the Innocents or "*Les Innocents*" for short), where Forum des Halles now sits, had accepted generations of poor and working class Parisians for ten centuries. It had accommodated so many bodies in fact, that the elevation of the cemetery had increased to eight feet above street level. It was also dangerous. In one fatal accident in 1780, underground workers were asphyxiated by toxic gases emanating from decomposing bodies improperly buried at *Les Innocents*.

Even above ground, odor was a constant nuisance, but it was the tracing of several deadly cholera outbreaks to cemetery runoff that prompted King Louis XVI to take action in 1786. And so it was that city planners came up with the idea to transfer the remains buried at Les Innocents, as well as those from over thirty other churchyard cemeteries and paupers' graves, to a large, abandoned quarry called Montrouge under Place Denfert-Rochereau. At that time, Denfert-Rochereau was on the outskirts of the city and not heavily populated. There would be little objection from the neighbors. Furthermore, since Les Innocents was located in the heart of the city, the majority of city residents would support moving this human toxic waste dump out of their backyard.

After the archbishop of Paris restored some measure of dignity to the dead by consecrating the quarry on April 7, 1786, grave diggers thus began the nasty task of disinterring millions of bones and rotting corpses. The wealthier deceased were marked by coffins; they had one. As for the homeless and working poor, for centuries their remains were put straight into the ground. But in April 1786, all was dug up, thrown helter-skelter onto horse-drawn carriages and moved under the cloak of darkness to Place Denfert-Rochereau.

There was no attention to detail. Whether pauper or nobleman, one's remains were dumped down an excavation shaft, all to end up in one big heap at the bottom. For those low on the socio-economic ladder in life, they had finally achieved equality in death, in the Catacombs. Once down below, the bones were carted away to separate sections of the quarry and artfully stacked up. The only form of identification given to the deceased was a plaque indicating the name of the cemetery from whence they came.

Remarkably, it took just over a year for the main transfer but then again, who would have wanted a project like that to drag on? It's hard to imagine public officials bickering over cost overruns or quality assurance while a cemetery in the heart of the city sat gaping open.

After Les Innocents was emptied and filled back in, out of necessity the Catacombs continued to receive the dead for the next eighty-five years. Though Paris continues to be plagued by strikes, most present-day tourists don't realize that for centuries, the City of Light was a dangerous and tragic place. Millions of residents died there prematurely from skirmishes, massacres and the many epidemics that swept across Europe. This fact is evidenced in part, by the need for a place to put all of the dead. There is no doubt that many of those whose scattered remains now rest in peace in the Catacombs suffered violent or miserable deaths.

"Dry Bones"

As she followed me down a circular staircase carved out of limestone, Charisse's first comment was, "Wow. This is *so* cool!"

Okay, so she wasn't going to freak out. Good. Once we got to the bottom and started to explore I tried, without much success, to translate the meaning of the many plaques and miniature alters that had epithets and poems carved into them. When you look at a map of the Catacombs it resembles an American suburban development. About one half mile long, the official tour steers visitors through winding tunnels that lead to cul-de-sacs. At each dead end (pun intended), one finds stacks or bins of bones that are arranged into linear patterns. Each section of the Catacombs traces back to a particular cemetery, but not always. Some of the bins contain the remains of victims of specific uprisings or battles from around the time of the French Revolution. In all, there are 13 markers along the tour, the purpose of each to name the source of the remains and to convey a sense of uniqueness – a proper thing to do given that in the case of the Catacombs, the deceased have lost all identity. Stacked within the bone arrangements are crosses, obelisks and stone tablets that have epitaphs carved into them.

The cemetery memorials are quite creative, if not schmaltzy. The Samaritan Fountain for example, the first point of interest on the tour, gets its name from the biblical verse, John 4:5-42, carved onto its face:

> Quiconque boit de cette eau aura encore soif. Mais celui qui
> boira de l'eau que je lui donnerai n'aura point soif dans l'eternité.

In English it says, "Whoever drinks this water will remain thirsty. But he who drinks water that I will give him will never be thirsty in eternal life." This quote was Jesus' response to a Samaritan woman who at first, refused to allow him to borrow her jar to draw water from Jacob's well.

Like all other subterranean fountains in Paris, water does not bubble forth from the Samaritan Fountain. That's because these "fountains" are essentially wells that tap into the *nappe phréatique*, the layer of water under much of Paris. Discovered by quarry workers centuries before, the aquifer provided them a ready source of water for cleaning their mining equipment and for keeping down the rock dust. It is not potable, though. The *Bain de Pied des Carrières* (foot bath of the quarries) is another well to the *nappe phréatique* within the Catacombs, but it was closed off to the public in 1995.

Some expected and also not-so-expected activities have taken place down in the Paris Catacombs over the centuries. Sacellum Crypt, one of the religious monuments along the tour, is a limestone alter where the church used to hold mass every year on All Saints Day. In the eighteenth century nobility both picnicked and held at least one formal dinner there. In fact, the Catacombs became such a fad among the upper classes that in 1811 they were officially opened for sightseeing, but only to those who had standing . . . . and probably the money to pay someone for the tour. It wasn't until 1874 that the Paris Catacombs were opened to the general public.

The author at the Sepulchral Lamp. A flame used to burn continuously in this stone dish in an effort to keep the air circulating. Photo by Charisse Fox

Since the names of the dead were lost in the move, historians can only piece together from gravestones and church burial records those whose remains are in the Catacombs. Based on those records, historians know quite a lot. Ironically, the remains of Paris' first Inspector General of Quarries, Charles Axel Guillaumot, are buried in the Catacombs. Ministers of government, cardinals, princes, French nobility and architects share their final resting place with Guillaumot. Somewhere in the stacks are the bones of French writers Rabelais, Racine, La Fontaine, Molière and Montesquieu; mathematician Pascal and political figures Danton and Robespierre.

A bump in the road

Charisse and I were walking down one of the long and narrow tunnels of the once-quarry when she stopped and looked up. Absently, I stopped and looked up too, though I didn't know at what. High up, maybe seventy or eighty feet, there was a white dome. Clearly there was daylight on the other side.

"Aunt Val, do you see that round white thing up there?" she asked, pointing to the daylight.

"Yes, I do," I said, gazing upward.

"Well, what's there?" she queried.

"What do you mean, 'What's there?'" I asked, obviously not getting it.

Rephrasing her question, she asked, "The round thing, the hole. What's on the other side of the hole?"

"It's an excavation shaft, I think. That's how they raised blocks of limestone to the surface when this used to be a quarry," I answered. Then I added, "It might be the shaft that they threw all the bones down into from the street."

"But what's at the top? . . . I mean, what's on the other side of the dome . . . up THERE?" she queried, pointing up again. I could tell she was getting frustrated with my failure to comprehend her question.

I thought for a few seconds, still looking up. Then it hit me.

"Ooh. You mean what's on the *other side* of the dome?" I said, arms folded across my chest in a thoughtful pose. I was proud that I had finally gotten it.

"I don't know . . . The street I guess," I answered matter-of-factly.

Charisse's brain was processing. After a few seconds she looked at me with a smirk and said, "You mean you're driving down the street in Paris and all of the sudden you hit a big bump and it's like, 'Oops, it's those goddamn Catacombs!'"

I laughed so loudly I might have awoken the dead. Several tourists approached us and as they did, they surveyed us with looks of disdain. Eyeing me, the elder, I could tell they were saying, "Respect the dead. How dare you laugh in such a place!"

Then, right at the moment that the court of disdain was passing us along the narrow tunnel, Charisse blurted out, "Just another bump in the road!"

I doubled over, cackling despite the quiet and the darkness that enveloped us, despite the blank stare of skulls, despite the fact that more tourists were approaching.

Charisse, in the meantime, was on a roll. "Oh . . . Sorry Aunt Val. Did I hit your . . . funny BONE?" she asked with a giggle. Then, "I guess you like my sense of . . . FEMUR!"

Still more: "Hey Aunt Val. You look chilled to the . . . BONE!"

There was no stopping her. Snapping her fingers to the beat she took it away, singing a verse from the old African American spiritual, "Dry Bones":

> Leg bone connected to the knee bone
> Knee bone connected to the thighbone
> Thighbone connected to the hipbone
> Don't you hear the word of the Lord?

Charisse in the Paris Catacombs. Photo by Valerie Broadwell

Charisse was getting out of control in the way that 19-year-olds do at Spring Break. Only we weren't in Fort Lauderdale, we were in a catacomb, and I wasn't nineteen anymore – though you wouldn't have guessed it. It was at this moment that my first epiphany of the day came to me eighty feet below Paris and it was this: I really hadn't changed much in twenty-plus years. Life – if you're lucky enough to have lived it – does indeed come full circle.

I found the epiphany comforting, so I just kept on laughing and as I was laughing, a Buddhist saying came to mind, though I don't remember ever having learned it. It was this, "Live life as if death were always on your shoulder." Contemplating reincarnation, I wondered whether in a former life I was a cave-dwelling, French-speaking monk. Surely that would explain why I found myself in this dark place in France, recalling a Buddhist saying that I don't ever remember learning.

My deep thoughts didn't last for long. In a laughing stupor, I tried hopelessly to force out, "Shhhh," but I had no breath left for speech. Rather, all I could do was contemplate in my head whether obnoxious foreigners had ever been thrown out of the place for disturbing the peace. Then a ridiculous question came to me, How do you throw somebody *out* of the Catacombs? Would a pack of security guards suddenly appear and carry us up all of those stairs?

Punch drunkenness and a mid-life kick of hormones drove my fantasies to new depths. I wondered whether Catacomb cops, called *cataflics* in the vernacular, were as cute as those foot police who patrolled the Métro in their sexy, peacock-blue suits. Like their subway counterparts, would the security guards for the dead be outfitted in those tight-fitting, designer jumpsuits – billy clubs and handcuffs dangling from their black leather belts in a proud display of machismo?

Then a second epiphany came to me that day, eighty feet below, and it was this: American chicks, wherever they are, pretty much think about the same two things – traffic and guys.

Eventually Charisse and I calmed down sufficiently to continue the self-guided tour with some measure of decorum. Giggling only here and there now, we lazily strolled through this valley of death. Lost in the moment, every few seconds we would gently collide into one another or one would trip over the other's feet because neither was looking where she was going. It was at this moment that a third (!) epiphany came to me and . . . Oh well, never mind. Women drivers.

It wasn't long before another question popped into Charisse's head.

"Aunt Val, since there are so many dead people in the Catacombs, how come it doesn't smell bad?" she queried.

Like I would know. I didn't have an answer so I simply told her, "Good question. I don't know."

I thought that Charisse's question was indeed a good one, so I posed it to the guard stationed at the end of the tour. Anxious for me to move on so that he could keep the exit vestibule clear, the guard's quick answer was that the remains were bleached with citric acid before being stacked up. His answer sounded suspicious to me, like something he had just made up on the fly. Was he telling me that they just pickled everyone? This being France, would they have thrown in some basil and rosemary?

I didn't then nor do I want to now, dwell on the subject of rotting corpses. However, the history of the Catacombs tells us that the remains entombed at Denfert-Rochereau weren't all fossilized bones from medieval times. Millions of those whose remains are in the Catacombs died in the eighteenth and nineteenth centuries – victims of the French Revolution, political skirmishes and epidemics. These political and natural events produced a huge number of casualties, so many in fact, that officials needed a place to put all of the bodies. The question is what did health officials do to the bodies so that they could be safely entombed in the Catacombs?

I did not forgot about Charisse's question nor the security guard's rather lame answer, though I could overlook it since it is altogether possible that he didn't comprehend my question. So months later, after I had already returned to the States from this particular research trip, I followed up with Sylvain, a veteran cataphile.

"The Catacombs do not smell bad because the bones are there for centuries!" [sic] he wrote in an email message. "Even in the unofficial parts, where bones are certainly not treated, it does not smell like anything. I guess they are too old, and really reach the fossil state," he concluded.

So it seems that this question shall remain another mystery of the Catacombs.

The "unofficial parts" that Sylvain was referring to are abandoned quarries beneath cemeteries that apparently became overflow space for remains that the living no longer cared about. Though I was not able to piece together the entire story, I am guessing that when grave diggers came upon fossilized bones in Paris' main cemeteries like Montparnasse and Montrouge, they moved the bones to quarries deep under in order to make room for new graves.

Though the secret ossuaries are closed off, the cataphiles have found a way into them. One of them is a forbidden section of the Paris Catacombs, near Denfert-Rochereau. Another, called *Carrefour des Morts* (Crossroads of the Dead), is under Montparnasse cemetery. Describing it Sylvain wrote, "Bones just lie there in an incredible mess."

Seasoned cataphiles go to the unofficial catacombs from time to time for kicks, taking pictures of themselves posing with skulls and bones, and then posting them at their websites – an activity that I find distasteful and very disrespectful of the dead. I once made my opinion known to one of the cataphiles whom I had befriended, scolding him for putting sunglasses and a baseball cap on a scull and then posting pictures of himself beside it at his website. My opinion was not well received.

Most of the churches in Paris have crypts in their basements where deceased religious leaders are remembered amid a somber and ornate backdrop – a stark contrast to the dinginess and anonymity of the Catacombs. There are also crypts in various places underneath Paris, but they are not usually open to the public. An exception is the Crypt of Notre Dame, a museum that lies directly beneath the plaza in front of the Notre Dame Cathedral. Seldom mentioned in Paris guidebooks, this archeological site contains artifacts and some human remains dating as far back as the time of the Parisii, a Celtic tribe who were the first to inhabit the area, settling on a muddy island in the middle of the Seine – later named Île-de-la-Cité. Unlike the Catacombs, the crypt of Notre Dame is not loaded with bones, so those with the heebie jeebies need not worry. The most interesting feature of the crypt of Notre Dame is that it tells the story of Paris development, layer by layer.

Don't you hear?

At the end of the Catacombs self-guided tour there is a bright red *Sortie* (Exit) sign indicating the way out. Even though we were having fun, both Charisse and I were relieved to see a sign of life. We had been in the Catacombs for nearly an hour – long enough to be in a place that is cold, damp and dark when sunny Paris beckons above. So with Charisse leading the way, I and another group of foreigners began our trek up the spiral staircase of eighty-two steps, a climb that takes a person in shape two to three minutes to get to the top. But since I was still having fits of giggles from Charisse's jokes, my progress was hampered. The group of tourists behind us was tailgating but unlike the first set that passed us along the tunnel, this group was younger and more light-hearted. Apparently, our humor was contagious because soon they began laughing too, even though we didn't even speak the same language. I think they were Italian.

Arriving at the top and out of breath, Charisse and I were anxious to feel the warmth of sunlight on our backs and to breathe fresh . . . well, relatively fresh . . . air. I was ready to take in more of Paris; to let her feed my senses.

We were ready to bolt out the door when we were called back by a guard who stood behind a table near the exit. Waiving his index finger at us he said in English, "You cannot leave." What I had forgotten from my last trip to the Catacombs was that before leaving, all visitors must have their bags checked for "souvenirs." It so happens that over the years, enough tourists had pilfered bones that decades ago officials began checking bags. What people do with stolen bones, I don't know. But if it were one of *my* ancestors, I surely would not want a piece of them displayed on someone's mantelpiece like a rack of antlers on a wall.

My heart was heavy with this thought when I slung my daypack onto the table and opened it for inspection. Grave robbing is the last thing I would ever do or hope that anyone else would do. So as I patiently watched the guard riffle through my things: notebook, French-English dictionary, Métro map, camera, wallet, bottle of water – a familiar tune crept into my head and it would not leave:

> Leg bone connected to the knee bone
> Knee bone connected to the thighbone
> Thighbone connected to the hipbone
> Don't you hear the word of the Lord?

. . . and so I left the Catacombs smiling.

I think the spirits were pleased.

Chapter 6

That Stinking Feeling

Every morning at 6:30 a.m. they descend into a murky, foul-smelling place where their job is to flush out the wastewater for a city of two million.[1] They encounter large consumer goods like car fenders and bed frames, but plenty of small stuff, too. The inventory garners great respect for the world's sanitation workers, wherever they are.

To protect themselves from the many hazards, sewermen wear full-length jumpsuits stuffed into hip-high rubber boots. They must always don a hard hat and protect their hands with heavy rubber gloves. In a French documentary one Paris sewerman reported with a chuckle, "These days we find condoms, lots of them, in all colors. Condoms and needles. They're all over the place."[2]

But the risks go far beyond contact with used condoms and sharps. Flash flooding can whisk a worker away to his death in minutes. A cut or open sore has the potential to cause serious illness since any break in the skin allows the bacteria, viruses, protozoa and microscopic worms floating in the water column direct entry into the body. In addition, sewer workers are regularly exposed to wastewater viruses such as HIV, hepatitis A and enterovirus, a super-virus that can manifest variously as polio, Coxsackie's, (hand, foot and mouth disease), meningitis and in rare cases, even encephalitis, a swelling of the brain.[3] *Escherichia coli* (E. coli), *Salmonella* and *Clostridium tetani* (the bacterium that causes tetanus), are three of the many bacteria typically found in sewer water and to which workers are also exposed. Then there are those nasty intestinal parasites like *giardia* and various amoebas.

This is the life of Paris sewermen, a cadre of about four hundred men who keep the city's over thirteen hundred miles of sewer lines flowing. Despite these dangers, a job working in the sewers is still sought after among laborers because of the shorter, 6 ½-hour workday, the higher pay and job security.

More than just @!$#

Finding matter other than doo-doo in a sewer isn't out of the ordinary for a big city like Paris. In 1935 a six-foot alligator was found living in a New York sewer. Nobody knows how it got there but the theory was that the reptile was flushed down a toilet while still a baby. It somehow managed to survive the journey through wastewater treatment and made it to the sewers where it lived on a diet of New York City rat. Yum.

Paris sewermen haven't encountered any alligators but there are plenty of other dangers in addition to exposure to biohazards, and overall, the risks seem to be increasing. Though the sewermen of prior centuries contracted killer diseases like tuberculosis[4] and cholera, today's workers are exposed to modern-day consumer hazards like toxic pesticides, hair dye (lots of it, based on the rainbow of hair colors up above), biomedical waste, engine fuel and toxic chemicals like benzene and toluene. Because fuel spills can show up in the wastewater at any time, it is not safe to operate engines lest a spark ignite and cause an explosion. The other reason for not using combustion engines in the sewers is that without adequate ventilation, carbon monoxide emissions from the engine could build up and suffocate workers.

What these limitations mean for sewermen is that much of their work still requires brute strength and stamina to pull wooden boats called *wagon-vannes* (flushing carts) and the larger *bateaux-vannes* (flushing boats) against the natural current of the underground canals.[5] Paris runoff in particular, contains so much sand and silt that without constant dredging it wouldn't take long for the underground channels of wastewater to completely clog up and stop flowing. The brainchild of Eugène Belgrand, the hydraulic engineer who, along with Haussmann, designed the present-day Paris sewer and water supply network, these *wagon-vannes* and *bateaux-vannes* trap debris so that the muck, sand and trash floating in the wastewater can be scooped out. The technique, developed in the nineteenth century, remains in use today with workers still employing Belgrand's boats to help them do their job. One major improvement since Belgrand has been the addition of mini-tanker trucks stationed over manholes at street level. Outfitted with hoses long enough to reach the channels below, the trucks suck up the sludge and debris trapped by the flushing boats so that sewermen no longer have to shovel it.

Drowning poses perhaps the greatest danger. To keep crews out of harms way, one worker is often posted at street level to maintain a lookout for the sudden rain showers common in Île-de-France. If the spotter sees dark clouds on the horizon, workers are ordered out of the water. As happens in the concrete Los Angeles River basin, even a far-off cloudburst can quickly change a slow-moving current into raging rapids, sweeping workers off their feet and fast away through a treacherous maze of obstructions and submerged objects. The scene wouldn't be unlike that in the 1998 film version of *Les Misérables* in which Jean Valjean (played by Liam Neeson) makes a quick escape down a manhole with the badly injured Marius. They dodge police bullets up above, but are almost drowned by a fierce current down below.

A closely knit society

Even though immigrants to Paris had broken through the employment barrier for other service jobs decades earlier, as late as the 1970s, Paris sewermen remained a closely-knit society of native Frenchmen.[6] Getting a job in the sewers without a family connection was nearly impossible, even when there was a flood of new hires during and after the Second Empire. Once in, however, workers were seldom fired and had access to a social network unlike no other in the service sector. Along with entry into the "club" came membership into a group that had a quasi-magical identity and its own code of ethics. Though France's socialist Fifth Republic (1959 to present) provides generous benefits to retirees, survivors and the disabled, this wasn't always the case. Before France overhauled its public welfare and retirement system, sewermen took care of their own, making up the difference between pitiful pensions and survival by subsidizing those in need with donations from working sewermen.[7] The generosity didn't stop there. Children of sewermen whose circumstances had left them orphaned were often adopted by other families of sewermen.[8]

Still, passing the hat and fundraisers couldn't keep up with a growing rank of retirees, widows and orphans of sewermen, so in 1905 the sewermen's union convinced the city of Paris to rent them seventeen acres of land along the Marne River for practically nothing.[9] Here they began building an agricultural colony with the intent of providing a communal home for sewermen and their survivors who could not otherwise provide for themselves. For roughly a decade, the nearly self-sufficient commune provided a home for those in need within the sewermen community.[10]

The colony was functioning but not yet complete when World War I broke out in 1914. The draft hit the colony hard, taking away the able-bodied sewermen who had been providing the free labor to build the colony. Most of them never returned.

Then, at the end of the World War I in 1918, there came another blow. The Germans ransacked the place before leaving France. The colony managed a comeback after the War, but only as a vacation getaway for sewermen and their families. The resort concept lasted until World War II when, during the Occupation, the Germans converted the space into a prisoner of war camp. The colony received its fatal blow when both German and French forces tore up the place at the end of the Second World War.

Life before sewers: Watch your step!

Though the Romans had built a state-of-the-art underground sewer system for Rome, contrary to popular belief, they didn't do the same for Paris. The first sewers in Paris were not underground but troughs that coursed down the middle of cobblestone or gravel streets – transit routes shared by pedestrians, street vendors and horse-drawn carts alike. The troughs are still visible today in the medieval towns scattered throughout France, many of which have changed little other than that they now have electricity, running water, flush toilets, garbage pick up and that ubiquitous curse of modern times: the automobile.

Back before there was public sanitation not only the streets, but cities in general, were stinky places. Waste of all sorts – cooking oil, human feces, horse manure, spoiled food and gray water – was poured either into the street, dumped into nearby streams or spread onto fields out back. Rain was the only agent to clear things out so that when there wasn't any the waste just sat there. One can only imagine the odor.

When there were downpours, hilly passageways became fast-moving streams of filth that were impossible to cross. In Paris the wastewater eventually settled into low-lying areas around the city, forming putrid lagoons that drew clouds of disease-carrying flies and vermin.[11]

Despite his many marital problems, King Philippe II Auguste, who reigned from 1180 to 1223, made significant, lasting improvements to Paris. Begun in 1163 before he was crowned, he wisely continued construction on Notre Dame Cathedral after becoming king. He commissioned construction of the Louvre as a fortress, as well as created the city's first central marketplace that functioned as such until 1979. Philippe Auguste left his footprint on the roads as well, paving the major thoroughfares through Paris. His road projects included installation of a central drain for wastewater coming off the street. Stone pavers were an improvement over gravel because when it rained, at least the waste on the streets could be diverted to brooks and smaller rivers more quickly. But the stench remained since the collector drain was at street level and the wastewater that didn't make it to the Seine or Bièvre Rivers settled and remained in the gutters.

It isn't clear, at least to me, when Paris got its first covered sewer, but the two dates I found are close. And although the sewers may have been very different structures, the initiators had the same idea. According to one source, Paris got its first covered sewer in 1325 under the Hotel Dieu.[12] Forty-six years later in 1371,[13] a city official must have had Rome on his mind when he convinced the government to construct a vaulted, underground collector sewer under rue Montmartre – one of the oldest streets in Paris that was laid out by the Romans. The collector sewer drained into the Bièvre River, possibly marking the beginning of the end of this ill-fated tributary that once coursed through the Latin Quarter.

Over time sanitation gradually improved, but often it was only after some type of human waste crisis. As early as 1530 property owners were ordered to dispose of their household waste into cesspools rather than dump the contents of their chamber pots and gray water directly into the street.

Once cesspools became common practice, the government only allowed them to be emptied at night. Cesspool workers, relegated to the very bottom of the social ladder,[14] made their rounds under the cloak of darkness,[15] emptying the cesspools into barrels – the contents of which ended up in either a huge city dump called Montfaucon or it was poured directly into the Seine. Because this haphazard system of waste removal continued to expose food and drinking water to human feces, infectious diseases like cholera and typhoid fever made periodic, lethal comebacks.

Cholera the driving force

Before Paris got its sewer makeover and the legendary sewermen to keep the system flowing, there was not only a prevailing stench throughout much of the city, there was also cholera, a water-borne disease that ravaged the population at least three times just in the nineteenth century alone. Most devastating was the epidemic of 1832 that killed twenty thousand people in and around the city. The primary route of exposure to cholera is hand-to-mouth contact, or the "fecal-oral route" that occurs when hands contaminated with feces (or vomit) from a victim pass the bacterium *Vibrio cholerae* to the mouth during eating, drinking or smoking. Sometimes all it takes is touching contaminated hands to the face. However, the general public believed that one caught the disease not through physical contact but by inhaling the odor of contaminated feces. It wasn't until the second half of the nineteenth century that public health officials began making the hand-to-mouth connection and realized that cholera could only be eradicated if sewage and drinking water were properly treated and simple hand washing with soap became habit. It was about that time, in 1850, that Belgrand began his huge undertaking to fix and expand the sewers.

Cholera is a brutal disease that can kill in hours, not days. Symptoms include profuse, watery diarrhea, vomiting and cramps. It is the rapid loss of body fluid brought on by the disease that leads to dehydration and shock. Without rehydration, death can occur quickly. Because a weakened immune system or malnourishment makes a person more susceptible to the disease, cholera hit the youngest and the oldest with vengeance. And although no social classes were immune, the poor were hit disproportionately hard because they lived under more crowded conditions where food, water and waste were in close proximity and hygiene was more difficult to maintain. Poor children, more likely to suffer from malnutrition than their middle- or upper-class counterparts, succumbed to the disease in great numbers. Fed up with government officials, healthcare professionals and the wealthy, whom they perceived as indifferent to their losses and suffering, poor and working class residents rioted in the streets for help.

The cholera epidemic of 1832 eventually slowed, but cholera reappeared in 1849[16] and again in 1892, even though Belgrand's sewers were in place by 1878. It was only after the third strike that public health officials were successful at convincing Parliament that the solution to ridding the city of cholera was to vigilantly remove human waste from the city and to keep it from sources of municipal water. With Belgrand's 373 miles of underground sewers in place, Parliament outlawed cesspools and required in 1894 that every building be hooked up to the new system so that all human waste would be quickly flushed out and away from the city. The government even created a slogan for their public health campaign, "*Tout à l'égout*" ("Everything to the sewer").

A city transformed from the bottom up

Belgrand's sewers were long overdue. At the outbreak of the French Revolution of 1776, Paris had only sixteen miles of sewers and by this time, they were so clogged up with centuries-old sludge that they were useless. Emperor Napoléon I (1804-1814) made some progress, adding nineteen miles of vaulted, underground collector canals. But his additions were undersized and inadequate for a city that was growing by leaps and bounds. Plus, without a system that provided for periodic flushing, the collector canals would eventually clog too.

However, Emperor Louis-Napoléon Bonaparte III (1852-1870) pursued urban renewal at a scale never before seen since the enormous projects undertaken by King Philippe II Auguste in the thirteenth century. Napoléon III's vision for the Second Empire was to transform Paris into a large, modern city, from the depths of the subway system to the top of the Eiffel Tower – and everywhere in between, including the sewers, railroad stations, the city's main outdoor market, the Garnier opera house and public parks. The emperor delegated much of the conception and planning to Baron Georges Eugène Haussmann (1853-1870), the creative but sometimes ruthless Prefect for the Seine. He was ruthless because of the many historic structures and entire neighborhoods that he leveled in order to make room for the wide boulevards that allow for multi-uses, but which would also give the military a strategic advantage to close off the city should rioting erupt. The narrow, winding streets of Île Saint-Louis and some pedestrian streets in the Latin Quarter are all that are left to convey the feeling of what all of Paris was once like, pre-Haussmann.

To fix the sewers, Haussmann named Eugène Belgrand Director of Water and Sewers. Working closely together, the two engineers figured out what needed to be done and how to do it in order to get the sewers working again. The task had three parts to it. The first was to unclog and rebuild the roughly one hundred miles of existing sewers to meet new standards. The second was to expand the sewers to every street in Paris so that the system could remove the wastewater from a city of one million, a figure that didn't even include Auteuil, Passy, Grenelle and Montmartre, villages just outside of the city that Haussmann would soon annex.[17]

The last task and the one that would have the most dramatic impact on public health was to bring uncontaminated water into the city from sources far upstream, store it safely and make it available to all residents.

Belgrand didn't disappoint.

They paved a dump and put up a paradise

Up until the time that Eugène Haussmann waved his magic wand and made it go away, Montfaucon was a notorious, odoriferous and hazardous dump in what is now the 19th arrondissement that received human waste from all over Paris.[18] Before cesspools were outlawed by Parliament, workers, arriving from a night of emptying cesspools, would wheel in their barrels of human waste and empty them into large settling basins. After settling out, the solids were spread over open-air fields where they cured for one to three years – for all the city to smell. Over time, the solids turned into a greasy, grayish-black powder called *poudrette* (fine powder), a fertilizer so potent that it was prone to combustion. Farmers from near and far came to buy it, and the *poudrette* was even loaded onto barges on the Seine so that it could be sold to markets downstream. Growers sprinkled the greasy substance onto their crops sparingly.

Slaughterhouses were also located at the site so that the combined stench of animal waste plus open air plots of decomposing feces made the city almost unbearable at times, especially on stagnant summer days when a foul plume hung motionless over the city. By the mid-nineteenth century odor pollution was probably intolerable on some days. Furthermore, Paris was slated to host the Universal Exposition of 1867. How could France showcase the artistic, industrial and architectural accomplishments of the Second Empire when the city smelled like an outhouse?

Convinced in 1860 that Montfaucon had to go, Napoléon III sent (who else?) to the rescue but master planner Eugène Haussmann. With his sweeping visions of a Paris with wide, tree-lined boulevards and leafy parks that functioned as public living rooms, Haussmann came through once again. After shutting down Montfaucon he commissioned Jean-Charles Adolphe Alphand to convert the wasteland – a rock quarry before it was a dump – into the lovely Buttes-Chaumont, a whimsical, hilly public park with the best view of Paris in town.

Another goop crisis

Although Belgrand's underground masterpiece was effective at both removing waste from the city and at providing residents with safe drinking water through a system of aqueducts and sealed reservoirs, his plan fell short in one critical area: wastewater treatment. Between 1800 and 1850 the population of Paris more than doubled in size from five hundred thousand to more than a million. New sewers alone, all of which emptied into the Seine, could not possibly meet the wastewater disposal needs of a city that was growing exponentially. The impact of the human population on the river became obvious when, at Clichy and Saint-Denis, two villages downstream, a huge, stinking mass of bubbling muck over one half mile long formed. The goo was so thick that it had to be regularly dredged so as to not block navigation along the Seine.[19]

With Montfaucon now closed, city officials still needed somewhere to go with ever increasing amounts of human, household and industrial waste, for it was clear that the Seine had reached its maximum carrying capacity. The city operated a human waste dump at Bondy but it was not adequate and it operated haphazardly; too much of what was dumped at Bondy ended up in the Seine as untreated runoff.[20]

The solution that followed around 1870 was filtration fields, or sewage farming – a technology founded in Scotland and which rapidly spread to several countries on the Continent. This ingenious approach to water treatment begins with separating the liquid portion of wastewater from the solid. The solids are made into fertilizer while the liquid portion that contains rich nutrients good for plants is used to irrigate crops. Sewage farming enabled the city to have somewhere to go with the sewage rather than dump it directly into the Seine. But the most impressive feature of this technology was that it allowed formerly barren fields surrounding the city to be converted into productive farmland so that they could provide a nearby source of fresh fruits and vegetables to city residents.[21]

Paris' first non-human waste farm was built in 1869 along the Seine, about five miles due north of the city at Gennevilliers.[22] Much larger sewage farms followed at villages strung along the Seine, which, after

World War I, filtered most of the wastewater from Paris.[23] Although the practice began to slowly decline as suburban land prices went up (and subsequently high levels of metals and other pathogens were discovered in the soil from all that dumping), the practice of using treated wastewater to irrigate both cropland and golf courses has actually been on the rise since the 1980s, mainly in the coastal areas of France where water is in short supply while the population is increasing.[24] Sewage farming is an interesting agricultural practice to contemplate while munching on a *salade Niçoise* in a Paris bistro. One wonders whether the vegetables with such good color and flavor were fertilized with wastewater from *la toilette*.

Nevertheless, don't let such thoughts keep you from eating raw fruits and vegetables in Paris. These days, all wastewater flowing out of Paris is piped to one of four wastewater treatment plants (WWTP) that service Île-de-France: Archères, Noisy-le-Grand, Valenton and Colombes. The oldest and largest of them at Archères has been expanded and upgraded several times since it was built in 1938. Today, Archères is one of the largest WWTPs in Europe. The sewer system itself continues to expand too, crawling ever outward to serve new development or to replace aging systems. Depending on what sources you consult and on which parts of the metropolitan area are included in the count, the network totals anywhere from 1,300 to 1,492 miles. To get a visual image of just how many miles of sewer there are under Paris, 1,492 miles is roughly the distance between Paris and Istanbul.

Sewer allure

I am the only person I know who has paid not once, not twice, but *three* times to see the Paris sewers. Strange as it sounds, the more I read about them, the more fascinated I became with the history, the engineering and the role that sewers have played in French culture. So I kept going back. The first time I toured the sewers it was in the late-1970s and I was with a group of my college peers. I can no longer recall the specifics but I do remember being slightly hung over from a previous night of carousing in the Latin Quarter. Given my physical state at the time, the sewers weren't really such a bad place to be. If I had needed to upchuck all I had to do was lean over the railing. Nobody would have cared.

Main gallery of the Museum of the Sewers of Paris. Photo by Valerie Broadwell

I didn't return to the sewers until the mid-1990s and by this time, the idea of writing a book about subterranean Paris was already on my mind, so I had ulterior motives for going back. I had been living in Paris for several months and although it sounds romantic and exceedingly fun the truth is, I was lonely a lot of the time. I was therefore always trawling for company on my weekend Paris jaunts – usually to obscure places. For this particular excursion I not only wanted the company, I needed the help of a French person who spoke English and who could translate some technical terms for me. Enter the picture, Philippe: pretty good English, native Frenchman, long-time friend and added to all that, an engineer by training. Perfect. The circumstances of my second visit read like another French play with a sewer twist. I can still recall the conversation I had with Philippe who was my *copin* (buddy), as opposed to my *petit ami* (boyfriend) – although I'm not sure the distinction mattered in this case.

We were having our typical weekend dialogue which consisted of me trying to convince Philippe that I just *had* to see or do something slightly weird like visit the Catacombs, eat steak tartare on the Champs-Elysées or drink a pastis at La Closerie des Lilas, one of several legendary hangouts of Ernest Hemingway and his avant-garde contemporaries. On this day my goal was to convince Philippe that going down to the sewers would be a really cool thing to do.

Philippe and I had maintained our transatlantic friendship for over a decade, so we obviously had developed a bond that spanned time and nationality. But the one significant difference between us was that he was only interested in spending his free time experiencing beautiful things that inspired, like art exhibits and outdoor music concerts under the ultra-modern Arche de la Défense. I couldn't blame him for this, though. After all, he was only being what he is: French.

Thinking back now on our conversation, I realize how unfair it was of me to expect him to be excited about going down to the sewers. Culturally, it was analogous to Philippe begging me to join him on a bus tour of New York City dumpsters. It went something like this:

"But why do you want to see the sewers?" Philippe asked me, puzzled by my enthusiasm.

"Because I want a T-shirt that says, 'I saw the Paris sewers,'" I answered sarcastically. (At one time there used to be a vendor who sold T-shirts that said, "*J'ai vu les égouts de Paris.*")

"If you want a T-shirt then just go buy the shirt. You don't need to go to the sewers. They just smell bad. Why pay money to see shit?" he snickered.

"I don't *really* want a T-shirt, Philippe," I snapped. "I want to see the sewers because I'm going to write a book about underground Paris. Remember?" Maybe Philippe really wasn't the adventurous type that I thought he was I contemplated, disappointed.

Still, I persisted. If I dropped the subject now my fear was that we would end up in some boring café in the Marais. What a waste of time *that* would be. Oh nooo, I wasn't about to let that happen. I just had to get up on my soapbox and lecture yet another Frenchman about his country.

"To Americans, the sewers are really cool. There's all that history, you know? *Les Misérables*, Haussmann, the Resistance hiding out, thieves escaping in them, the mysterious sewermen. There isn't anything like *les égouts* in the U.S." I continued, ad nauseam.

Philippe wasn't buying it.

"I thought Americans came to Paris see the Eiffel Tower, Montmartre, the Louvre and the Notre Dame. But I was wrong. The truth is, they come here to see the sewers," Philippe answered, straight-faced.

Throughout our conversation we were sitting on a wall overlooking the Seine. After Philippe's last comment I solemnly put down my head and remained silent for a good minute in a gesture of surrender. Our disagreement wasn't really about the sewers but about the camaraderie between us. I had met Philippe in 1983, right after finishing a two-year stint as a Peace Corps Volunteer in Morocco. We had remained friends ever since. This time, Philippe was bailing on me, and he knew it. So, possessing a sixth sense for knowing when to play French, I kept my head down and pouted my frosty pink lips. The wind whipping off the Seine blew my curly, highlighted locks into my face and his, so that Philippe had to brush away my hair from his face and as he did he smiled, chuckling to himself. Now he was the one who had the look of surrender. The French actress Julie Delpy would have been so proud of me. I was the perfect typecast female lead in a French romance: fragile, submissive, exceedingly feminine, irresistible.

Oh, and one more thing: clever.

Fifteen minutes later Philippe and I were standing in line at the entrance to the sewers, waiting to buy our tickets. Two hours later we were sitting at a lovely outdoor café in the Marais, me picking up the tab for two cold, beaded glasses of Stella Artois. The sidebar lesson: the company of a Frenchman can be bought . . . cheap.

The last time I went to see the sewers I didn't even try getting someone to go with me. I wanted to go alone. I was in Paris specifically to conduct research for this book so going anywhere by myself was no longer something I dreaded but rather, an experience to be coveted.

In fact, on my third visit to the sewers I was so busy taking notes and pictures that I lost track of time and stayed until closing time. A guard had to remind me to leave. It is remarkable how ten years and two kids later my sense of self had so dramatically changed to the point where going anywhere alone – even the Paris sewers – was a treat, not a pity party . . . Ah, but maybe that's my next book.

The dialogue between Philippe and I is just one example of the Paris sewers providing the setting for a good story – mine with a happy ending. Let us not forget Victor Hugo's landmark political novel. In *Les Misérables* only the thieves knew their way around the Paris sewers, the hotbed for Hugo's dark and powerful underclass that would one day rise above the privileged rich.[25] The fact that only the thieves knew their way around the labyrinth of tunnels under the city wasn't that far from reality. As late as the 1830s city officials didn't even have a comprehensive map of the sewers. To research the setting for his novel Hugo hired civil engineer H.C. Emmery, head of the Paris sewer system from 1832 to 1839, to help him navigate this unchartered territory, which the writer used as the backdrop for several key scenes.

The Madwoman of Chaillot by Jean Giraudoux (1942) is another literary work that centered on the Paris sewers.[26] In this play, unlikely heroes bond together to save the city from a band of greedy oil speculators who are convinced that black crude flows through the sewers of Paris. Quite a stretch but maybe worth a revival given that global politics of the twenty-first century are now completely driven by the stuff. Think of the ramifications if oil were indeed discovered under Paris.

Though it was still a work in progress, Paris first began offering tours of its famous sewers during the Universal Exposition of 1867. Described as an engineering triumph, Eugène Belgrand's new and vastly expanded sewers and water reservoirs dramatically reduced the occurrence of many water-borne diseases but most importantly cholera, a disease that had killed so many. The public health success of the sewers explains, in part, the public's fascination with and appreciation for the sewers – from health experts, to writers, to the bourgeoisie and eventually, to tourists. Today, over one hundred thousand people a year file through the Museum of the Sewers of Paris. The humble entrance is easy to miss because it's only a small kiosk along the Seine River at the corner of

Pont-de-l'Alma and Quai d'Orsay. One American reporter described the entrance as, ". . . what looks like a big manhole on the sidewalk."[27]

Flush with pride

Despite whiffs of Parisian wastewater which is very much what one would expect in a sewer, though not unbearable, the Museum of the Sewers of Paris provides insight into the consequences of such everyday activities as taking a shower, running the dishwasher or flushing the toilet – modern-day conveniences that residents of developed countries take for granted. It also includes stories and photos of some interesting items that have turned up in the sewers. Reportedly, a lot of teeth make their way down drains and end up in the sewers, as do keys. The remains of an orangutan were once discovered in the sewers. The ape had gone missing from a city zoo, apparently making its escape via an open manhole. If only the poor thing had been able to read the street signs below it might have found its way back to the zoo . . . or a train station.

Every Paris sewer line is marked with the name of the street above. Photo by Valerie Broadwell

Besides teeth, keys, the unfortunate orangutan and according to one source, even a crocodile[28] (though not known whether dead or alive), there are rats down there – lots of them. So many in fact, that the sewer guides like to point out a shocking estimate about the City of Light: there is one rat living below Paris for every human living above. The rodents pose yet another risk for sewer workers because when cornered or startled, the animals are known to become aggressive. When they attack humans, the little monsters go for the hands and face, delivering deep bites that carry all sorts of germs, creating wounds that are prone to infection.[29]

The rats aren't all bad, though. According to the museum guides, they consume a whopping fifty percent of the solid waste floating in the waste stream, thereby helping to keep things flowing. One doesn't want to contemplate what exactly it is that the rats are eating, but for me at least, the question remains: Are not the rats simply recycling what is already there? After all, for living creatures what goes in, comes back out. So where does all that rat poop go?

It is at this point that the waste cycle begins to curve back toward its source. I am thinking of the sewage farms and those colorful, tasty *salades Niçoise* that so many of us have enjoyed with a hunk of fresh French bread and maybe a glass of chilled white wine in a Paris bistro. If you find disgusting the thought of that nasty brew and all those rats floating only fifteen feet below from where you're sitting, here's one positive way of looking at it: If you live in Paris or even just visit, every time you flush, you've become part of a grand circle of life that gives, takes and then gives back again. So when you flush, do so with pride, for you've become part of something bigger and greater than us all.

The Paris sewers are unique in the world for several reasons. A large part of why the sewers are so impressive is because of Haussmann's rigid interpretation of how collector streets should look and function. He wanted wide, straight and tree-lined boulevards that provided unobstructed views of national monuments from end to end. Telephone, electrical and other utility lines would clutter the view so he instructed Belgrand to design a sewer system that would accommodate (thus hide) as much urban infrastructure as possible. Consequently, the sewers carry a lot more than just wastewater. In fact, they provide for the transport of three types of water: potable, non-potable[30] and of course, wastewater. In addition, the tunnels also contain miles of compressed air pipes, natural gas lines, telephone cables and even pneumatic tubes that were once used by the postal service to send letters. Later, when traffic lights were added to the streets, the sewers were used to house the wiring.

Sheer size and scope are also what make the Paris sewers stand apart from other systems around the world. The main canals are wide and deep enough to accommodate a small boat. What's more, every sewer line was built tall enough to allow an adult to walk upright so that workers don't have to get down on all fours to make repairs or to inspect. Because of their multi-functionality, height and the sheer vastness of the system, the sewers have been used by both good and evil forces throughout history. The Nazis used them for air raid shelters during the Occupation, but the Resistance took advantage of the sewers, too. They held clandestine meetings under the cover of the sewers and hid some of their weapons cache there, too. Hundreds of sewermen were available to the Resistance as foot messengers. Working as a relay team, they could pass messages from one underground Resistance hideout to the next.[31] At the end of the War, when street fighting broke out as the Allied Forces approached Paris, the Resistance set up a first aid station for injured fighters in a gallery under rue Gay Lussac in the 5th arrondissement.

In more recent times, bank robbers have used the sewers as an escape route once they got the loot. It is rumored that at one time, Paris police patrolled the sewers underneath the Iranian Embassy, suspecting terrorists might use the sewers to escape with hostages.

The sewers mirror the street grid above so well that each tunnel is marked with a corresponding street sign. What's more, the address of every building appears next to where the building's waste enters the system. This precise signage enables sewermen to easily navigate their territory city block by city block and know exactly where they are. In fact, they know their beat so well that, if given notice early enough, they are able to retrieve valuables such as rings and necklaces that go down the sink or the toilet either unintentionally or otherwise. Armed with only an address, they can nail the point of entry and start searching there. Ever since hearing this factoid from a sewer guide I've often wondered how many engagement or wedding rings have been flushed down the toilet in the heat of a lover's quarrel, only to be retrieved by sewermen after the couple made up.

Flushed with pride, I imagine the sewermen shaking hands and giving each other 'atta boy slaps on the back. Wide grin on his face one says to the other, "Yep, another marriage saved, all in the line of duty."

Notes

1. The population of just the twenty arrondissements of Paris is about two million. However, the entire Paris metropolitan region, called *Île-de France*, is approaching eleven million.

2. Françoise Marie, *France: Beneath Paris* (Derry, New Hampshire: Chip Taylor Communications, 1998).

3. Although both the polio virus and HIV (human immunodeficiency virus) are commonly present in wastewater, the risk of contracting either from contaminated wastewater is very low, according to several publications cited at the Center for Disease Control website (http://www.cdc.gov/index.htm). See "Exposure to Biohazards," by Donald J. Garvey, *Professional Safety*, August 2005.

4. Donald Reid, *Paris Sewers and Sewermen: Realities and Representations* (Cambridge: Harvard University Press, 1991), 154.

5. Ibid., 30. Paris sewers flow using only the force of gravity. Designing a system that relied solely on gravity wasn't that difficult to do since the Paris basin slopes downward from its highest point in the northwestern 19th and 20th arrondissements, to its lowest point in the southeast, or roughly the 15th arrondissement.

6. Ibid., 132.

7. Ibid., 159.

8. Ibid., 160.

9. Ibid., 163.

10. Ibid., 163-165.

11. Reid, *Paris Sewers and Sewermen*, 12.

12. Alain Clément and Gilles Thomas, *Atlas du Paris Souterrain: La doublure sombre de la Ville lumière* (Paris: Parigramme, 2001).

13. The source of this date is the Museum of the Sewers of Paris.

14. Reid, *Paris Sewers and Sewermen*, 92.

[15] Ibid., 88.

[16] It wasn't just Paris that was hit. The Asiatic cholera pandemic of 1846-63 struck most parts of the world, including all of Europe, North Africa and North America.

[17] At the time of this annexation Haussmann created the twenty arrondissements, or districts, that still define the city limits of Paris.

[18] Reid, *Paris Sewers and Sewermen*, 11 and 72.

[19] Ibid., 75-58.

[20] Ibid., 78.

[21] Ibid., 62-65.

[22] Ibid., 60.

[23] Ibid., 65.

[24] François Brissaud, "Wastewater Reclamation and Reuse in France," Hydrosciences, MSE, Université Montpellier II *http://tierra.rediris.es/hidrored/ebooks/ripda/bvirtual/articulo06.PDF.* (accessed September 5, 2006, chapter in forthcoming book).

[25] Victor Hugo, *Les Misérables*, translated by Charles E. Wilbur. (New York: The Modern Library, 1992). Although *Les Miserables* is associated with Belgrand's sewers, Hugo began writing it during the years of the July Monarchy (1830-1848), well before the sewer expansion of the Second Empire.

[26] Ibid., 128.

[27] Alan Riding, "The Sights Beneath the Sidewalks," *The New York Times*, July 12, 1992.

[28] Cash Peters, "The Sewers of Paris: Bad Taste Tour," *The Savvy Traveler. http://savvytraveler.publicradio.org/show/features/2000/20000311/sewers.shtml.* (accessed January 19, 2005).

[29] Reid, *Paris Sewers and Sewermen*, 150.

[30] The nonpotable water, pumped directly from the Seine, is used to wash down the sidewalks and to water public gardens.

[31] Reid, *Paris Sewers and Sewermen*, 52.

Chapter 7

"Oh Great Sea"

Yes, that's it. Grief. It's what I feel when the jumbo jet I'm buckled into rumbles down the runway at Charles de Gaulle International Airport, reaches the critical speed at which it becomes miraculously airborne and I lose contact with French soil. The pilot circles the airport until the aircraft is headed on a southwest path. Engines groaning, the wings slice through the clouds and smog of Île-de-France, climbing ever higher until we reach the unearthly lower stratosphere, the sub-zero, oxygen-deprived layer just above the troposphere at which most jets fly for better fuel economy. We will chase the sun all the way home.

France is not home but, like a child saying goodbye to his mother before a long separation, I feel a terrible emptiness whenever I leave her. Why? I don't know. On this day once we cleared the Continent, the sky became so clear that even through more than seven miles of air and space I could see ships, even whitecaps, on the deep blue sea. I was grateful for the peacefulness and beauty of this flight, for it helped to offset my sadness. Like I always do, within minutes of take – off I began sketching out a plan for how and when I would return.

I watched solemnly out the window as first the Continent, then England, and finally the last specs of Ireland drifted past until there was nothing left to look at but water. Knowing that we wouldn't see land for at least the next four hours, I hauled out my laptop from the overhead bin, fired it up and tried to tap out meaningful words for this chapter. Only I couldn't. My writer's voice had left me; something had chased her away. She wouldn't return until I allowed her back in, a decision that only the subconscious part of the brain can make. Until she came back, my keyboard would be useless. So I packed up the laptop and switched to a set of Air France headphones. While channel surfing past the muzak, the jazz, the classic and the country western music, I stopped when I heard the song "One Tree Hill" by U2.

After noting the station number on the dial, I went back to staring out the double-pane, frosted window, mesmerized by all of that space between the Earth and me. Perhaps I was overwhelmed by the contrast between the small, dark places I had been exploring and writing about for so long, and this seemingly infinite and bright openness. I wondered whether a cataphile might be terrified of flying, not for fear of crashing, but because his comfort zone is deep down within the Earth. The cataphile has a need to hole up and feel grounded. There is nothing more opposite than being suspended forty thousand feet above the earth, ungrounded.[1]

At the very end of "One Tree Hill" Bono sings the refrain for the last time. Sung *a capella*, it is sad, hymn-like and it goes like this:

> Oh, great ocean
> Oh, great sea
> Run to the ocean
> Run to the sea

I heard these words while my eyes were fixed on the ocean and in an instant, my writer's voice was back. I wanted her to stick around so, to the irritation of the British woman next to me, I scrambled out of my seat and got my laptop back down from the overhead bin.

"Would you please make up your mind?" she grumbled under her breath in the Queen's English.

Returning to my tiny allocation of airspace, I yanked down the tray table, fired up the laptop and began tapping:

> It was the gift of tiny marine creatures, showered upon the
> ocean floor for millions of years that created what's known

among geologists as the "Paris basin." The deposits left behind after the shallow ocean receded provided the perfect blank slate for the Seine to sculpt its curvy, sensual course through the basin and eventually, out to the sea.

The gift of time, ocean pressure and layers of marine sedimentation were also the ingredients needed to make limestone – a resource that humans learned early on to use in creative ways. Without such deposits the world might not have a Notre Dame Cathedral and its gargoyles, the Garnier Opera House, the Louvre, the Arc du Triomphe, the remains of a Roman amphitheater, nor even the lovely bridges that span the Seine. Why not? Because the most striking buildings and structures in Paris (save for the Eiffel Tower) are made of limestone blocks that came right out from under the city or from quarries nearby. The empty spaces left after the limestone was removed have, in turn, earned their own place in Parisian history and culture.

So there it was: the womb of Paris right under me. Archeologically speaking, it was the ocean that gave us Paris as we know it, both at its surface and below. No wonder I couldn't stop staring at it.

Will there always be Paris?

Subterranean Paris is crisscrossed with a maze of tunnels, galleries and extraction shafts – the scars that remain after centuries of mining. Combined, the area totals over nineteen hundred acres. Added to that are over one thousand miles of sewer lines that snake their way under the city this way and that, as well as hundreds of miles of subway tunnels, 380 subway stations, underground parking garages – even an entire underground shopping and community center at Les Halles. At times, I couldn't help but wonder whether there was anything at all holding up the city. Might Paris one day fall into an abyss?

I'm betting that it won't.

Although Paris probably has more hollowed out space underneath it than any other city in the world, most of it still stands on solid ground. Recall that way back in 1777, after a series of building and street collapses, the *Inspection Générale des Carrières* (Inspection General of Quarries or *IGC*) was created to map out the quarries and to find the weak spots. The galleries and tunnels at risk were strengthened by adding supports or by simply filling in the cavities, a remedy called *injection* in French. In fact, so much repair work was done back then that it is relatively rare to find a tunnel wall older than the eighteenth century. In general, only the quarry ceilings date back further. Most of the extraction shafts that were once scattered throughout Paris have been filled in or capped.

The Inspection General of Quarries at 1, place Denfert Rochereau. Photo by Valerie Broadwell

More than two centuries later, the IGC still repairs the quarries as needed, but only those under public land and structures: streets, government-owned buildings and parks. They do not inspect nor maintain the quarries under private property. Surveying subterranean Paris is serious business. At least one Paris neighborhood, the village-like Butte aux Cailles in the 13th arrondissement, can never be heavily developed because its substratum is gypsum – too soft to support the weight of large buildings. In other areas where buildings were unknowingly or carelessly built over quarries centuries ago, pillars have been added to bridge the gap between the foundation and the quarry floor. If you looked at a cutaway of one such building it would look like a beach house on stilts except in this case, the stilts would be made of stone and they would be much taller than those of a beach house.

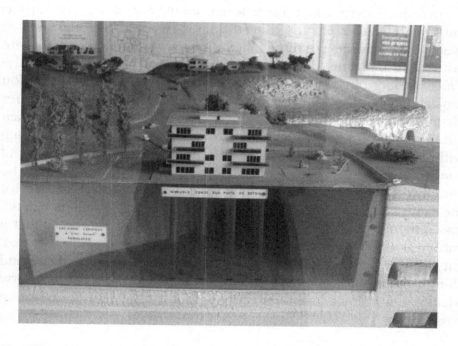

This miniature model located in the lobby of the IGC shows how buildings constructed over abandoned quarries are supported. Photo by Valerie Broadwell

In addition to ongoing survey and repair work, the IGC must also approve building permits, oversee the Paris Catacombs and regulate open-air quarries outside of the city that are still actively mined. Although they probably don't wish to advertise it, one of the IGC's most important functions is keeping maps of the underground up-to-date. Because the maps are produced with taxpayers' money, the public cannot be prohibited from purchasing them. Cataphiles regularly buy the IGC's maps, edit them according to their own discoveries and then circulate the doctored up maps to the cataphile community via the Internet. So, in an ironic twist of duty, the IGC keeps the maps current in part, so that the cataphiles don't get lost or injured doing what they're not supposed to be doing in the first place. Legally, those who go poking around the underground do so at their own peril. But the IGC knows that if their maps weren't current, a lot of cataphiles would quite literally be in deep trouble.

In truth, if there is anything to fear, it should not be of losing Paris to the abyss but rather, of Paris losing the abyss. According to one estimate, every year an average of three miles of quarry tunnels and quarries are lost due to injection, deliberate closures or new construction. In the 1960s, underground history sustained a blow with the modernization projects aggressively pushed and approved by then-Prime Minister Georges Pompidou. In particular, acres of ancient quarries were taken out to make room for the fifty-nine story Montparnasse Tower. Along with the monolithic building came a shopping center and underground connections to the subway and to Montparnasse train station. The complex functions well as a commercial and transportation hub for the southwest side of the city, but to this day cataphiles still mourn the loss. The out-of-proportion skyscraper caused such an uproar that a ban on skyscrapers within Paris city limits was subsequently imposed. City leaders came up with an alternative plan to locate all of the tall and shiny buildings northwest of the city at La Défense, just beyond Porte Maillot. One glance in that direction and it is clear that the proposal passed.

As for the subway, plans are in place to extend Métro Lines 12, 13 and 14, all of which will tunnel under the city. Luckily, extension of Line 14, the Météor, from the Saint-Lazare station south through the 13th arrondissement did not impact Paris' second largest underground quarry (the one I toured with the cataphiles).

Following a worldwide request for proposals, city officials selected a design proposed by David Mangin to give Forum des Halles and the surrounding neighborhood a makeover. As of this writing work has not begun pending major revisions to the proposal and neighborhood input. Given that the current Les Halles generally got a thumbs down from locals, there is no telling what the new one will look like – or how badly it will tear up one of the city's oldest quarters, second only to Île-de-la-Cité. Since municipal elections are in 2008, it is doubtful that any ground will be broken before then.

There is no doubt that, little by little, the quarries, bunkers and legendary party rooms – many which bear striking works of art or have significant historical value – are being lost to make room for new subway lines, additional sewer lines, underground parking garages, shopping centers or whatever else the ingenious French decide is a good thing to put below ground.

Who knows? Maybe as the government struggles to accommodate an ever-growing population, some Parisians might decide that a subterranean apartment would be a fine place to live. Think of what it could offer compared to an apartment on a noisy boulevard: quick access to the subway, no traffic noise, less heating in the winter, cooler in the summer. And if underground housing were built right beside a place like Les Halles, just like the characters in the movie *Subway*, one could live underground for weeks without ever having to surface . . . except maybe to walk the dog.

Since these fascinating, subterranean open spaces will diminish as the City of Light grows and evolves, cataphile wannabes might want to experience subterranean Paris before more of it is lost, either to collapse, closure or a new building. Some of the places I've written about are not open to the public so I can't advise you to go there. Readers are reminded that going down a manhole to explore the quarries is illegal, not to mention dangerous. It was only a stroke of good luck and probably good French that got me an invitation to a five-hour tour with experienced cataphiles, or landed me in the basement of the Garnier Opera House where I got to test the waters of the phantom's "lake."

Having said that, there are still plenty of underground places open to the public all year round such as the Museum of the Sewers of Paris and the Archeological Crypt of Notre Dame. Passionate underground enthusiasts who want to maximize their subterranean sightseeing should plan a trip around *Journée du Patrimoine* (Journey of Inheritance), a national, week-long event in the fall when the government allows access to extraordinary underground sites normally not open to the public. But English speakers be warned: the tours will be in French. Also be aware that a reservation is needed in order to get a spot on most *Journée du Patrimoine* tours in the Paris area.

Happily, two historical sites I've written about have been or are in the process of being restored. The Paris Catacombs were closed to the public from January to May 2004 for major renovation. Given the care that the IGC puts into maintaining this unique site, duties which include, among others, keeping moisture levels down, preventing cataphiles from breaking in and tourists from stealing bones, it is clear that the government recognizes the Catacombs as a national treasure to be kept and protected for the sake of historic preservation, if not tourism.

In addition, the Bièvre River, little sister to the Seine, is slowly becoming uncovered and rediscovered. Several associations offer walking and cycling tours of the Bièvre outside of the city where it eventually emerges into the open air. Even within the 13th and 5th arrondissements through which this ancient brook once coursed, residents have proposed several sites for restoration, one of them Kellerman Park and another near the Gare d'Austerlitz where the Bièvre originally joined up with the Seine.

Following are links to sites I've written about in this book, as well as to organizations which offer the opportunity for a legal and safe descent to subterranean Paris. I've also provided links to the two largest cataphile websites: "cyberkata" and "CKZone" where you can post messages . . . maybe even make a cataphile friend or two.

Where to begin

Journée du Patrimoine
www.journeesdupatrimoine.culture.fr/
Notes: This is your best shot at seeing underground places not normally open to the public. The sites vary by year but previous program agendas included a tour of an RER control room, private burial crypts and a glimpse of the Romanesque Montsouris reservoir. The architectural tours of Métro stations offered in 2004 were booked solid.

Underground Waterways
Arch of the Bièvre River
30 bis rue du Cardinal Lemoine
Phone: 01 44 41 16 20
Métro: Cardinal Lemoine
Notes: The remnants of an ancient arch that once spanned the Bièvre are in the basement of the post office located at this address (Poste de Jussieu). The arch was once open to the public the first Wednesday of the month but at last check that was no longer the case. There are maps of walking tours along the Bièvre outside of the city at *www.bievre.org/*

Canal Saint-Martin
www.canauxrama.com/e_index.html
Métro: Jaurès
Notes: The open-air tour boats ply the canal every day except January 1.

IGC (Inspection General of Quarries)
1, place Denfert Rochereau
Métro: Denfert Rochereau
RER: Denfert-Rochereau
Notes: The IGC has a small museum in their lobby. It's free and open to the public on Mondays, Wednesdays and Fridays from 9:00 a.m. to noon.

Museum of the Sewers of Paris
Place Résistance face au 93 quai d'Orsay
www.v1.paris.fr/en/visiting/SITE.ASP?SITE=02036
Métro: Alma Marceau
RER: Pont de l'Alma

Paris Catacombs
1, avenue du colonel Henri Rol_Tanguy
www.v1.paris.fr/en/visiting/SITE.ASP?SITE=02027
Métro: Denfert Rochereau
RER : Denfert-Rochereau

Métro
www.ratp.fr/

Notes: Métro does not offer tours to the public on a regular basis, but you can certainly take a self tour. It's easy, cheap (just the cost of a subway ticket) and you can stay in the system until it closes at 1:00 a.m. If you can read French, the walls of Saint-Paul Métro station are covered with text and photos on the history of the Métro. The two oldest Métro stations in Paris are Porte Maillot and Porte de Vincennes on Line 1, but neither have interesting architectural features. My top five picks are La Bastille (both the above ground and underground sections), Les Abesses (take the stairs, not the elevator), Arts et Métiers, Cluny-La Sorbonne and Concorde.

Finally, for everything-transportation, stop by RATP's very cool gift shop at Châtelet-Les Halles. The boutique is located at the transfer point to the RER, near the place Carrée exit. www.souvenirs-metro.fr/

Forum des Halles
http://en.forumdeshalles.com/vue/form/forumdeshallesuk/accueil/accueil.htm
Métro: Les Halles or Châtelet
RER: Châtelet-Les Halles
Notes: Exit the subway station into Les Halles and just start wandering.

Quarries
The *Carrière des Capucins* (Capucins Quarry) under the Hôpital Cochin is the only quarry that one can legally tour through the Association SEADACC.
www.seadacc.com/
Métro: Saint-Jacques
RER B: Port-Royal
Notes: You may have to join SEADACC in order to get a tour. Emails sent on several occasions requesting information were never responded to.

Archeological Crypt at Notre Dame
http://en.parisinfo.com/museum-monuments/299/crypte-archeologique-du-parvis-de-notre-dame-de-paris?1
Métro: Cité
RER: Châtelet-Les Halles or Saint Michel-Notre Dame

Notes: Located under the square of Notre Dame Cathedral, this underground museum is billed as the largest archaeological crypt in Europe. The museum tells the story of how Paris began on Île-de-la-Cité and then developed outward from there.

Associations

l'Organisation pour la connaissance et la restauration d'au-dessous-terre (*OCRA*) (Organization for the Knowledge and Restoration of the Underground) 11, rue Barrault 75013 Paris
www.ocra.org
Information on guided tours: http://www.ocra. org/fichiers/ OCRA_Visitesguid ees.pdf
Notes: Founded in 1992, OCRA is a membership organization that promotes the preservation and restoration of underground sites, as well as arranges tours of underground sites that are of historical or cultural significance. Their tours, led by volunteer experts, are of educational nature only. You may have to pay dues and become a member in order to sign up for a tour which will most likely be offered only in French. Every year OCRA coordinates the underground site visits for *Journée du Patrimoine*, which are very popular. One year more than 750 visitors toured two restored nineteenth century underground micro-breweries near Paris.

Collectif de Port-Mahon et de la Ferme de Montsouris (Collective of Port_Mahon and the Montsouris Farm)
http://collectifportmahon.blogspirit.com/
Notes: This is the umbrella group of many clubs, all who have an interest in preserving and in some cases restoring, subterranean Paris – from rock climbers to history buffs.

Cataphile websites
www.cyberkata.org/
www.ckzone.org
Notes: There are hundreds of cataphile websites where they post pictures and stories documenting their descents. "Cyberkata" provides a good summary of all the different underground sites. "CKZone" is an electronic message board that anyone can join for free. You can post messages in French or even in English. Either way, chances are good that someone will respond.

The heart and soul of Paris

For centuries, the abandoned quarries beneath Paris have drawn a rainbow of characters into the darkness: imaginary and real, good and bad, young and old, dead and alive. The one thing they all have in common is a story to tell.

In the thirteenth century, bandits hid themselves and their loot in a quarry under what is now the Jardin du Luxembourg. Sorcerers and persecuted Catholics alike were known to hold secret masses in the underground. Before the French Revolution farmers and sellers of goods used the quarries as a secret passageway into the city, thereby avoiding the king's high taxes imposed on their produce and wares at the entrance gates.

After the fall of the short-lived socialist Paris Commune (from March to May 1871), Communard fighters sought refuge from President Adolfe Thiers' "Versaillese" troops in Père Lachaise Cemetery. But the rebels were trapped by the soldiers, lined up against the cemetery wall and shot dead. Throughout a bloody week of skirmishes in May 1871, the bodies of thousands of Communards were dumped in an open grave at the foot of the wall which later came to be known as the *Mur des Fédérés* (Wall of the Confederates). Today a large plaque in Père Lachaise marks the wall and commemorates the 147 men who were executed there on May 28, 1871. Another group of Communards reportedly retreated to the Paris Catacombs for cover but the Versaillese tracked them down and massacred the last remaining defenders of the Paris Commune right there in the Catacombs.

During the German Occupation of France in World War II, there is no doubt that the Resistance had an edge over the Nazis when it came to using the Paris underground for clandestine activities; the French had been navigating their subterranean backyard for centuries. They used the network not just for cover from air raids and German patrols, but as an effective means of communication. They avoided detection by tapping into telephone wires strung along the sewer lines or by sending human messengers through subway and sewer tunnels to other Resistance cells scattered about the city.

The Germans exploited subterranean Paris too, but their reach was limited. They infiltrated relatively little of the vast quarry, sewer and subway networks. All that's left now are the remains of two elaborate bunkers under the Latin Quarter – *le bunker du lycée Montaigne* (Montaigne High School bunker) and *l'abri des Feuillantines* (Feuillantines' shelter), named after the street above, but also known as *l'abri Laval*, as in Pierre Laval, the French politico who collaborated with the puppet Vichy government put in place by the Germans during the Occupation. *L'abri Laval* had toilets, showers, central heat, telephone service, a kitchen, a system to circulate air and even poison gas detectors, but it was built late in the War and never came to be occupied by the Germans.

After World War II students from the Latin Quarter began exploring the abandoned quarries with a lighter mission: recreation. Despite a November 2, 1955 law that declared the abandoned quarries forbidden territory, throughout the 1950s, 1960s and 1970s urban explorers and partygoers went down anyway, taking advantage of easy access from the basements of houses, buildings and public staircases that were put in during the War for civil defense. Medical students were known to scavenge for skulls in unmarked ossuaries where the remains of relocated cemeteries had been dumped centuries earlier.

The students gave names to large galleries like *Salle Z* (Room Z) and *la plage* (the beach) where they staged huge parties with live music. Since sound can't travel through sixty to ninety feet of limestone, fun seekers could literally hold a rock concert under the city and nobody at street level would hear a thing. By the 1970s cataphiles had jury-rigged electricity to Salle Z, making it possible to power up electric guitars, amplifiers, microphones and lights. With nearly three hundred access points, baby boomers were going down in droves. It was also during this time that "leader" cataphiles separated themselves out from the partying pack. Small groups of cavers and spelunkers began meeting regularly in the quarries not to party, but to explore and document unchartered territory.

During the 1980s, stories about this relatively unknown activity started making their way into the popular media. "Cataphile" became the mainstream word used to describe those who prowled the dark underbelly of Paris. The regulars started using pseudonyms to make it harder for the authorities to identify them. In 1983, the documentary book, *La cité des cataphiles: mission anthropologique dans les souterrains de Paris*[2](The city of cataphiles: an anthropology mission in the Paris underground) popularized clandestine exploration of the quarries. Together, literature, the media and soon after, the Internet, transformed what had been regarded by most as a creepy and dangerous activity limited to weirdos or drug addicts, into a hobby that garnered intrigue and curiosity. Once copy machines became easily accessible, novices began venturing down wielding reprints of the IGC's maps. Within a short time, stumbling around subterranean Paris was the "in" thing to do, and not just by students. Now that the world knew about the secret "city" underneath Paris, cataphiles were being contacted by people from all over the world who were asking to be taken down for a tour.

Was this the real heart of Paris, the underground? Indeed, throughout history subterranean Paris has always had a beat of its own. Now, authorities felt it needed to be stopped; it had gotten too loud and threatened public safety and government security. The IGC responded with an aggressive campaign to seal off as many access points as they could find.

A quarry needs air

The effect was suffocation. The IGC's massive closure of manholes, staircases and other accesses may have limited the number of people crawling around under Paris, but it created a new problem, stagnant air. The result has been an increase in the moisture content of the ambient air in the quarries. Cataphiles call attention to the money that the IGC has had to spend on dehumidifying the Paris Catacombs just to keep moisture from further deteriorating the bones. They go so far as to equate each additional blocked gallery or tunnel with an incremental increase in humidity. In addition, the trash and stones left behind by careless "neo-cataphiles," those who go down for fun and leave their messes behind, blocks water flow. Because limestone is a porous rock, it absorbs water so that instead of flowing out of the tunnels and down into the *nappe phréatique*, rain and spring water that naturally seeps into the quarries is trapped. Tiny fissures form as the limestone, gypsum and clay expands and subsides with varying amounts of moisture, thereby weakening it. The effect, according to cataphiles, has been an increasing number of gallery and tunnel collapses. The collapses, combined with urban development, mean that the abandoned quarries are perhaps being lost at a rate faster than at any other time in modern history.

A quarry collapse under Paris. Photo by David Deschamp

Whether in online chat rooms, blogs or in conversation, cataphiles and historians express concern over the loss of a history and culture unique to Paris. The galleries and tunnels in particular, are a side of the city seen by few foreigners but important to an increasing number of Parisians, whether they be cataphiles, spelunkers or history buffs. One contingent of cataphiles wants the underground preserved for social reasons. They organize meet ups at designated access points, descend together, hike some, socialize, take pictures, then leave the quarry as they found it. These social-but-responsible types have websites and chat rooms where a core group of cataphiles shares news about closures, vandalism and accidents (usually someone falling or getting hit by falling rock).

Other groups like OCRA want to preserve the fountains, abandoned bunkers, breweries and legendary party rooms for present and future generations. The spelunkers go down for sport. Whether for social, recreational, historical or cultural reasons, the one goal these diverse clubs all have in common is a desire to preserve subterranean Paris from further loss. In fact, those with a stake in the underground have recently joined forces to form one umbrella organization called *Collectif de Port-Mahon et de la Ferme de Montsouris* (Port-Mahon Collective and Montsouris Farm).

By 2005 the number of access points within Paris city limits had dwindled from an all-time high of over 300, to a mere eight. This is a big change from the 1950s, 60s and 70s, when cataphiles were able to secretly enter the quarries via stairwells and basements. Now going down is a very public, illegal action. Recall that when I went down for my tour we entered through a manhole in the middle of a sidewalk on a busy boulevard just off place de l'Italie. Visibility hasn't stopped the cataphiles but it does put them at greater risk of getting caught by the police. Furthermore, with manholes as the only available points of entry, those who object to underground exploration can tip off the IGC on the location of an unsealed manhole. The result could well be one less access point.

The beat goes on

Since the 1990s injection has become the IGC's preferred solution as opposed to building up the hollowed space with supports. Not surprisingly, the cataphiles strongly object to injection as a fix because it completely destroys whatever underground structure there once was. Adding insult to injury, the injected site becomes another blockage that the cataphiles must then work around. But since these urban explorers are breaking the law when they descend, they don't exactly have a voice at the IGC.

An injection is the IGC's preferred method of shoring up a collapse. Cataphiles object because it makes the tunnel impassable. Photo by Stéphane Mezei

Despite ongoing battles with the IGC, the police and neo-cataphiles who vandalize or get lost, the experienced cataphiles are a tenacious lot. As my cataphile contact, Stef, defiantly told me during an interview, entering the quarries is only illegal within Paris city limits, so if the cataphiles are shut off from the city, they'll simply enter from outside the city limits where there are more access points and it's not explicitly illegal. The cataphiles have also been known to pry open sealed manholes, tunnel through blocked connectors or even circumvent IGC injections. So it seems to me that, try as they may, the IGC will never be able to completely stop the infiltration.

Times have clearly changed since the first wave of students began descending to the underground with the sole purpose of partying. These days, cataphiles complain on their blogs and websites about the media's failure to give them fair coverage. Instead, they claim the media focuses only on the sensational or the bizarre. The message that cataphiles would like to put out there is that subterranean Paris is a place worth saving.

For example, the Aug. 23, 2004 discovery of a movie theater under Trocadero, right in the shadow of the Eiffel Tower, made international news. Built by a group calling itself the "Mexican Perforation," these cataphiles cleverly tapped into underground utility lines for power and even siphoned water off the Trocadero fountains. Admittedly, the complex was a remarkable discovery worth reporting on, but so too is the historic value of the underground network as a whole.

The cataphiles I interviewed told me that the group who built the Trocadero complex were skinheads and for this reason, they kept away from that area, which is under the tony 16th arrondissement. Other than the audacity of it all, the real story is that there are now so many people prowling the underground that they have separated into factions, some of which have begun laying claim to territory. This attests to both the vastness of the system and a resurgence in the popularity of urban exploration as a form of recreation – maybe even a cultural phenomenon of the twenty-first century.

My story of the underground ends here, in Chapel Hill, North Carolina, but the stories of subterranean Paris go on, underneath the City of Light. Another writer could go to the same sites I went to and find a whole different set of characters, all with stories worthy of telling. I first descended to the underground with a writer's curiosity, but that's not to say I didn't also have great trepidation, especially during my first descent into the darkness with the cataphiles, with no bottom in sight. But I emerged (eventually!) feeling the magic that is down there. The cataphiles, the firemen who watch over the phantom's "lake," the people who operate the Metro, even the sewermen – I think they, too, feel the adventure, mystery, artistry, history, sadness and uniqueness of subterranean Paris. I hope I have done justice to the people I have met while exploring the dark side of Paris, whether dashing for a subway train, taking a hula hoop lesson, feeding the fish under the Palais Garnier opera house or bellying my way through a wet, clay tunnel. These experiences have enriched my understanding of a city that I thought I knew well. As readers have probably figured out, this book isn't really about the places I've explored, but about the people I've met along the way. So many welcomed me into their underground world and told me their stories, freely telling about the wonders of what they knew and saw, or gave me insight into what their lives were like either working or playing under the city. Best of all, they shared with me, knowingly or not, a bit of who they are. For this, I am all the richer.

I hope you are, too.

À la prochaine.

Notes

1   Transatlantic aircraft traveling eastbound fly at odd altitudes of up to 41,000 feet, depending on weather conditions and traffic, while westbound aircraft (i.e., that flying to the U.S. from France) fly at even altitudes, or up to 40,000 feet.

2   Barbara Glowczewski, *La cité des cataphiles: Mission anthropologique dans les souterrains de Paris* (Paris: Librairie des Méridiens, 1983).